the
INSIDE
JOB

How Jesus Can Transform
Your Personality

DAVID O. DYKES

FLUENCY
TELLING STORIES THAT MATTER

Produced with the assistance of Fluency Organization, Inc.
Graphic design: Inkwell Creative

Printed in the United States of America
Visit www.ncourageresources.org

INTRODUCTION

The events of June 17, 1972, launched our country into a constitutional crisis where the president of the United States, Richard Nixon, faced impeachment for a cover-up. That warm evening in June began with the arrest of five men for breaking into the Democratic National Convention headquarters at the now infamous Watergate complex. The men were later proven to be directly tied to the official organization of Nixon's re-election campaign, and taped conversations inside the Oval Office revealed Nixon's attempts to cover up the crime. Nixon resigned the presidency in August two years later, preventing what would most certainly have been his impeachment.

Watergate is a classic example of an "inside job" because the brazen act came from within Nixon's own camp. The burglary was not a random occurrence or sponsored by any outside foreign entity. An inside job typically describes a person in a position of trust operating from within and using special insider information to sway a situation toward a certain outcome. Although we typically think of this phrase in a negative way, this book explores the greatest "inside job" in history—the incredible transformation that takes place inside the heart of a Christian. When Jesus is living in you and displaying His personality, He works within you to produce radical change from the inside out. It is the ultimate "inside job."

The Bible shows us where God is at work—deep inside of us. "For it is God who is working in you both to will and to work according to his good purpose." (Philippians 2:13) Where is He working? Inside your heart and mine. Why is He doing that? So that we will not only *want* to do His will but also have the ability to do it. He transforms our personality into someone who wants to obey God with all our heart. There is a certain way in which Jesus works to accomplish this, and that is what *The Inside Job* is all about.

I once heard someone say about an obnoxious man, "That guy needs a personality transplant." Well, the truth is, we all need a personality transplant. We need Jesus to transplant His personality into ours. Today you can go into a hospital and get a kidney transplant, a liver transplant, a lung transplant, and even a heart transplant. The good news is you don't have to go into the hospital to get a personality transplant.

When you place your faith in Jesus, He comes to dwell in your heart through the person of the Holy Spirit. And if you surrender to Him, He can demonstrate His personality in you.

I think we can all stand to undergo some changes to our personality—who we are at the deepest level—so that we can be more like Christ, don't you? I hope you'll enjoy reading this book as much or more than I enjoyed writing it for you.

Pastor David O. Dykes
Fall 2018

CONTENTS

CHAPTER ONE

The Inside Job

One of the largest and oldest grapevines in the world is just outside the city of London. It's called the Great Vine at Hampton Court. It was planted in 1768 and some of the branches are over 200 feet long. A custom-designed greenhouse protects the vine year-round. It only has one trunk, or main vine, which is a whopping 12 feet in diameter, is essential to the hundreds of branches that receive life-giving nourishment from the vine, and workers harvest about 800 pounds of delicious grapes each year.

But many other branches on this massive vine only grow leaves without producing fruit. Those branches, although they are lush with beautiful green leaves, aren't firmly attached to the main trunk. A vinedresser will tell you that a leafy branch only has a superficial attachment to the vine and is a hazard in the vineyard. Therefore, each year they are cut off and burned because they compete with the fruitful branches for the life of the vine.

To me, that's a parable of religious people versus true Christians. Religious people have a lot of leaves to adorn their lives. They attend church and are often fluent in religious language. They talk about the Lord, but they only have a superficial attachment to Him. However, when you see real fruit in the life of a person, you know that they have a living relationship with Jesus.

What do people see when they inspect the "fruit" or results of your relationship with God? What kind of attitudes and actions is a Christian supposed to demonstrate when Jesus is inside of them? Because Jesus sent the Holy Spirit to live in believers and to represent Him, He is essential to how Jesus changes someone from the inside out. In fact, there are nine qualities that are present in the life of someone who is living in the power of Jesus. These are often called the fruit of the Spirit and they are listed in Galatians 5:22–25:

"But the fruit of the Spirit is love, joy, peace, patience, kindness, goodness, faithfulness, gentleness, and self-control. Against such things there is no law. Those who belong to Christ Jesus have crucified the sinful nature with its passions and desires. Since we live by the Spirit, let us keep in step with the Spirit."

It's important to understand that there is only one fruit of the Spirit. Did you notice the noun is singular—it doesn't say "fruits"? There is one fruit, but there are nine flavors of that fruit listed in Galatians 5:22–23. You may have seen a popular roll of candy called Lifesavers. It's a roll of different colors of fruit-flavored candy— orange, cherry, grape, etc. One roll of Lifesavers has many flavors inside. The same is true with the Spirit-filled Christian—one Spirit and nine ways that He operates in your life.

Many believers know WHAT these nine traits are, but sometimes they are clueless about HOW this fruitful personality can be displayed in their lives. I've heard some people refer to it as "The Secret to a Fruitful Life." But it's not a secret at all: in fact, it's simple. It's an INSIDE JOB when you understand that the key is Jesus living inside of you.

The truth is found in the teaching of Jesus about the vine and the branches in John 15. Jesus said, "I am the true vine, and my Father is the gardener. He cuts off every branch in me that bears no fruit, while every branch that does bear fruit he prunes so that it will be even more fruitful. You are already clean because of the word I have spoken to you. Remain in me, and I will remain in you. No branch can bear fruit by itself; it must remain in the vine. Neither can you bear fruit unless you remain in me. I am the vine; you are the branches. If a man remains in me and I in him, he will bear much fruit; apart from me you can do nothing." (John 15:1–5)

Jesus spoke these words the night before He was crucified. He knew His time left on earth was short. He would be crucified, resurrected, and after 40 days would ascend back to His Father. The disciples would no longer have Jesus physically present with them. But Jesus promised them something—Someone—even better. He promised He would send the Holy Spirit to live in the disciples, and the Holy Spirit would bear witness to Jesus. He would empower the believers to demonstrate the personality of Jesus, the fruit of the Spirit.

To launch a nuclear-powered missile from a submarine, both the Captain and his First Officer must insert two keys into the launch director and turn them at the same time. It takes both of those keys to launch the missile. When you combine the key of John 15 with the key of Galatians 5, you are ready to launch out in the exciting adventure of life full of the fruit of the Spirit! Here are four life-changing truths that Jesus shared about living a fruitful life.

TRUTH #1: FRUIT IS PROOF OF MY RELATIONSHIP WITH JESUS

When you buy fruit in the grocery store, you see a little sticker on it. That means somewhere between the tree and the store, someone at the USDA inspected that piece of fruit. When it comes to people, Jesus said we are all to be fruit-inspectors. In Matthew 7:16 He said, "By their fruit you will recognize them."

God's plan for your life isn't that you'll be successful. Instead, He wants you to be fruitful. What is the difference? Jesus said, "This is to my Father's glory, that you bear much fruit, showing yourselves to be my disciples." (John 15:8) The best way you can live a life that gives glory to God is to bear much fruit. Jesus said that your fruitfulness is PROOF that you are His disciple. We sometimes say, "The proof is in the pudding." When it comes to the Christian life, the proof is in the fruit!

Christian fruit is expressed in two different ways. In one sense, the fruit of a Christian is another Christian. It involves spiritual reproduction. Let me explain what I mean by examining an everyday item in most kitchens. Inside an apple there are apple seeds, and in each seed there is the potential for an apple tree that will, in turn, produce many more apples. God's first command to Adam and Eve was to "Be fruitful and multiply." That's still God's plan for us—that we should be involved in leading other people to faith in Jesus Christ. That's spiritual reproduction.

The reason churches exist is because someone planted Gospel seeds in the lives of people who planted more seeds of the Gospel. And as a result, we're experiencing the harvest of fruitful Christians who have come before us. Are you planting seeds of the Gospel wherever you go? Can you point to someone and acknowledge that you planted the seeds of the Gospel into their life? The fruit of a Christian is another Christian.

But the Bible gets even more specific. Spiritual fruit also describes the nine personality traits found in Galatians 5. Fruit is simply the outward expression of the inner nature. Some people can tell a tree by its leaves or bark, but I can't. But when I see and apple hanging on a tree, I know that's an apple tree. It has the inner nature of an apple. When I see an orange hanging on a tree, I say, "That's an orange tree." When I see spaghetti hanging on a tree, I say, "That's a spaghetti tree." Just kidding. Spaghetti doesn't grow on trees...it grows on bushes, I think.

TRUTH #2: I CAN'T PRODUCE FRUIT—I BEAR THE FRUIT JESUS PRODUCES

There's a difference between producing fruit and bearing fruit. Think about it. A branch just shows off the fruit the vine has produced. Jesus is the vine, and I'm the branch. If you get that backwards you're headed for spiritual fatigue and frustration.

Some well-meaning believers treat these nine personality traits as a daily to-do list. They say to themselves, "Today I MUST be completely loving, totally joyful, absolutely peaceful..." And they go all the way through the list. If you're like that, then you're setting yourself up for frustration and failure. Branches don't produce fruit:

they only bear fruit.

MEMORIZE THIS

"No branch can bear fruit by itself; it must
remain in the vine. Neither can you bear fruit
unless you remain in me." (John 15:4)

The biggest mistake you can make regarding the fruit of the
Spirit is to think you can manufacture love, joy, peace, patience,
kindness, goodness, faithfulness, gentleness, and self-control. Fruit
can't be manufactured. You'll never see a fruit factory. You might
see a factory that cans or processes fruit, but you'll never see workers
making fruit from scratch. There are factories that make cars, clothes,
and computers but not fruit. Fruit comes naturally when there is a
proper mix of water, sun, and soil nutrients. It comes supernaturally
when there is a proper mix of the Life of the Son, the power of the
Holy Spirit, and your willingness. In the illustration Jesus uses of a
vineyard, He is the vine. His Father is the Gardener, and we're the
branches. Where's the Holy Spirit? Jesus didn't say it, but it would
make sense that the Holy Spirit is represented by the life-giving sap
flowing from the roots into the vine and then into the branches.

A village leader from a remote area of Nepal once visited a modern
city for the first time. He was fascinated by the electric lights, a basic
amenity of modern life that he had never seen. He was amazed that
he could flip a switch on the wall and a small ball of glass in the ceiling
would shine brightly. With the little money the village had given
him, he then went into a hardware store, bought a few light bulbs,

and a plastic wall switch. He packed them carefully in his suitcase and returned home.

When the other villagers saw his strange items, they asked him what they were. He smiled and proudly announced, "Just wait until dark, and you will see." The members of the village gathered that night and watched the man tie the small balls of glass to the underside of the thatch ceiling in his hut. He next affixed the plastic switch to a wood beam by the door. Finally, he said, "Watch this!" And he flipped the switch with a dramatic flair. Nothing happened. Again he flipped the switch, only to be disappointed. What he didn't know was that the switch and the bulbs were useless unless they were connected to a source of power.

Trying to demonstrate the nine expressions of the fruit of the Spirit on my own is like that man trying to make lights shine with no power. Fortunately, we have access to the Holy Spirit—the supernatural power source required to create love, joy, peace, patience, kindness, goodness, faithfulness, gentleness, and self-control.

My friend Ron Dunn understood this truth. He wrote: "A branch is just a grape rack that God has there to hang His fruit on. My responsibility isn't to produce fruit; my responsibility is just to be available for God to hang His fruit on me."

TRUTH #3: BRANCHES THAT ARE PRUNED PRODUCE MORE FRUIT

When you examine Jesus' words carefully in John 15, you see He mentions three levels of fruitfulness. He speaks of bearing fruit, then he mentions bearing MUCH fruit, but there's a third level that He called MORE fruit. There is only one way for a vine to produce more fruit; it has to be pruned. Jesus said, "Every branch that does bear fruit he prunes so that it will be even more fruitful." (John 15:2)

Imagine you get to the place in your Christian life where you are walking in the Spirit. You have surrendered control of your life to Jesus, and people start seeing evidence of all nine personality traits in your life. What comes next? Do you think you'll get a blue ribbon or a trophy? Not quite. The Divine Gardener comes along and looks at your life. He smiles, and then He does something totally unexpected. He pulls out a pair of giant clippers and He begins to cut away parts of your life.

One difference between a beginning gardener and a master gardener is that the more experienced gardener understands fruit trees and grape vines have to be pruned back in order to produce the most fruit. That's counter intuitive. You would think you'd do everything you could to keep the tree branches and vines growing longer and stronger, but if you never prune them, they don't produce fruit.

Do you know what you call an apple tree that's never been pruned? A shade tree. I know. We have one. Early on, there were a few small apples, but we decided we needed the tree to shade one of our windows, so we never pruned it. Today it's a large, leafy tree, but it no longer produces apples.

On the other hand, I also have a grapevine growing on an arbor. Every winter I prune off all the old branches. I cut them back all the way to the main vine. If you looked at that vine after I pruned it, you would think I had killed it. But every summer it grows more grapes than we can eat. The difference? Pruning.

Pruning is painful. When the Lord starts pruning our lives, we want to say, "No, Lord, not THAT! Don't take that away! Don't cut that!" But the loving Gardener says, "I'm doing this because I love you so much that I want you to bear even MORE fruit."

The best apples I've ever tasted grow on the slopes of Northern Israel near the Syrian border. Israeli Druze villagers have transformed the once barren mountainsides into orchards with hundreds of apple trees. Each one is loaded down with apples, so much so that some of the branches must be propped up. My friend Reuven Solomon, who is our group's tour guide, told me about a visit he made to one of those orchards. He was surprised to see gashes and gouges on the trunks and larger branches. Concerned, he asked the farmer what happened. The apple farmer had discovered that if a healthy apple tree wasn't producing much fruit, they would cut the trunk and slash the bark with large knives. There was something in the tree that responded to those wounds, and the trees became much more fruitful. The farmer even admitted that the trees with the most scars produced the most fruit.

I've known many Christians who bear the scars and gouges from emotional, relational, or financial pain in their past. Oh, you can't see these scars, but these men and women have been pruned in many ways. And yet, they aren't bitter or angry. They are some of the most loving, joyful, and patient people you've ever met. They understand the value of God's pruning.

In fact, one of the most fruitful servants in the history of Christianity was the Apostle Paul. Do you know what *Paulos* means in Greek? It means "little one." We'd translate it "shorty." Stature was not his only shortcoming. When you read the Book of Acts you see that his life was full of pain and adversity. In other words, God did a lot of pruning in his life. But it was the Apostle Shorty who started so many churches and wrote over half the books in the New Testament.

In 2 Corinthians 11 Paul mentions just a few of the hardships he endured. He writes, "I've been flogged five times with the Jews' thirty-nine lashes, beaten by Roman rods three times, pummeled with rocks once. I've been shipwrecked three times and immersed in the open sea for a night and a day. In hard traveling year in and year out, I've had to ford rivers, fend off robbers, struggle with friends, struggle with foes. I've been at risk in the city, at risk in the country, endangered by desert sun and sea storm, and betrayed by those I thought were my brothers. I've known drudgery and hard labor, many a long and lonely night without sleep, many a missed meal, blasted by the cold, naked to the weather." (2 Corinthians 11:24–27 *The Message*) Most of us would love to be used like Paul, but do we really want to be pruned like Paul?

TRUTH #4: YOUR MAIN RESPONSIBILITY IS TO REMAIN FIRMLY CONNECTED TO JESUS

John 15:5 has become one of my life verses. This is where Jesus said, "I am the vine; you are the branches. If a man remains in me and I in him, he will bear much fruit; apart from me you can do nothing." (John 15:5) Apart from Jesus I can't be loving. Apart from Jesus I can't be joyful. You can go down the list of all nine flavors of the fruit of the Spirit—I can't do any of them on my own. Jesus said that my responsibility is to remain in Him and He will do the rest. The King James Version says, "Abide." It's the word *meno*, which means to stay connected to. Jesus uses it 10 times in just a few verses.

J.C. Ryle captured the idea when he wrote: "When Jesus said,

'Abide in me' He meant, 'Cling to me. Stick fast to me. Live your life in close and intimate communion with me. Cast your whole weight on me. Never let go your hold on me for a moment."

The best word to describe this type of relationship between a branch and a vine is dependence. I am dependent on Jesus to allow His life to flow through me. The branch (me) is just an extension of the vine (Jesus). Sometimes we reverse that picture and live as if we're the vine and Jesus is the branch. We have our plans, our goals, our priorities, and we attach Jesus to our lives. The problem is that Jesus doesn't work that way. We want Him to be an attachment to our life; but He wants to be our life.

I've known a lot of Christians through the years who are struggling, striving, moaning, and groaning to live the Christian life. They develop spiritual hernias from struggling too hard to be fruitful. "Ooooh," they say, "I'm going to love that person if it kills me! I'm going to be joyful today if it kills me!" And it almost does. My advice to that type of Christian is to relax. I've spent a good bit of time working on my grapevine at home, and I've never seen one of the branches sweating or heard one groaning to produce a grape. Instead they're just up there hanging with the vine.

How good are you at juggling? Through the years I've practiced, and I can juggle three balls pretty well. The world record for juggling at this time is 13 balls. But the guy was only able to catch each ball once! Could you imagine trying to juggle nine balls? Imagine working with the love ball, the joy ball, the patience ball...and then you've still got six others to manage. Scripture advises us that there is just one ball to juggle: abiding in Christ. Remaining in Christ. The principle is to stay dynamically connected to Jesus. When I just concentrate on that one priority, the result is that all nine of those "balls" start circling my life like planets in orbit around the sun.

What does it mean to abide in Christ? Let's start with what it is NOT. To remain in Christ isn't a passive act of sitting in a lotus position and humming. It's not expecting Jesus to take possession of your personality and you become a zombie. It is an active seeking after Jesus with your whole heart. It is staying in constant contact with Him. You do this through developing daily habits like prayer and memorizing and quoting Scripture as Christ does His work inside of your heart to transform you into the kind of person He wants you to be.

Psalm 1 describes a person who meditates on God's Word day and night. That person's life radiates success and contentment. The psalmist says that person is like a tree planted by the rivers of water whose fruit does not wither. Once you decide to start actively abiding in Christ, you'll be busier than you have ever been. But you won't be busy doing a hundred different things; you'll be doing one primary thing—abiding in Jesus.

Do you feel a little guilty because you don't recognize much evidence of the fruit of the Spirit in your life? Let me share something profound about fruit. Fruit grows over time. Have you ever walked up to an orange tree with no oranges, and then while you're staring at it, "Pop!" a fully mature orange suddenly appears? Fruit grows slowly, and if you don't yet have a fully mature set of all nine flavors of the fruit of the Spirit, it just means God is still working on you. I know He's still working on me.

When I was serving in my first full-time church after seminary, I faced a lot of discouragement. I didn't have any joy in preaching and serving. I felt like a failure. I was doing everything in the strength of my own flesh, and I was worn out mentally and spiritually. I was seriously considering getting out of the ministry and applying to medical school. I even checked into taking Organic Chemistry classes at a local college, because I knew I'd need that to score well on my MCAT test. This was in 1978 and somebody gave me a cassette tape of an unknown preacher named Charles Stanley. It was a message from John 15 on how to live a fruitful life. Then I read a little book by Major Ian Thomas entitled *The Saving Life of Christ*. God used the truth from John 15 and Ian Thomas to change my approach to life. I learned the foundational truth that I didn't have to live the Christian life; Jesus is available to live His life through me. What a difference that has made.

Major Ian Thomas served in the British Army during World War II. He was a decorated hero who received the flag of surrender from the German army. He was also a perfectionist, a soldier's soldier who lived strictly by army regulations. After the war, he set out to devote that same sense of obedience and perfection to the Christian life. He was determined to be a perfect Christian, but he was constantly frustrated because he continually found himself unable to be Christlike in all his actions and reactions. He was on the edge of spiritual burnout when he fell on his face before the Lord and they had the following conversation.

"The Lord said to me, 'For seven years, with utmost sincerity you have been trying to live for Me, on my behalf, the life that I have been waiting for seven years to live through you. Since that day you have given mental consent to the truth that I have been in your heart and have accepted it as a theory. But you have lived

totally ignoring the fact. You have been busy trying to do for Me all that only I can do through you.' I learned to say, 'Lord Jesus, I can't—You never said I could. But You can, and always said You would.'"

Try praying that prayer: "Jesus, I can't. You never said I could. You can. You always said you would!" I can tell you that four decades after I discovered this truth, I'm more excited about serving the Lord than ever before. Will you be willing to pray that prayer today? That's the secret to a fruitful life.

TAKEAWAY TRUTH
Put What You're Learning Into Practice

Starting tomorrow, why don't you take five minutes in the morning, or at some other time, and simply read God's Word? Ignore everything else and just imagine yourself attached to Christ like a branch is stuck into the vine.

CHAPTER 2

Love: The Greatest Of All

As a reminder, fruit is the outward expression of an inward nature. Remember, an apple tree bears apples. An orange tree bears, you guessed it, oranges. When you see a red or an orange piece of fruit hanging from a tree branch, you know what kind of tree it is. When these nine personality characteristics are activated in your life, it is the evidence of Jesus living in you.

Love Is Key

In this chapter, we'll examine love, the first fruit on God's list. There's a lot of confusion about what love is. A group of children were once asked to define love, and here are some of their answers:

Karie, age 5, said: "Love is when a girl puts on perfume and a boy puts on shaving cologne and they go out and smell each other."

Emily, age 8 said: Love is when you kiss all the time. Then when you get tired of kissing, you still want to be together and you talk more."

Karen, age 7, said: "When you love somebody, your eyelashes go up and down and little stars come out of you."

Mary, age 6, said: "Love is when your puppy licks your face even after you left him alone all day."

Lauren, age 5, said: "I know my older sister loves me because she gives me all her old clothes and has to go out and buy new ones."

Jessica, age 8 said: "You really shouldn't say 'I love you' unless you mean it. But if you mean it, you should say it a lot. People forget."

More songs have been written about love than any other topic in the world.

Olivia Newton-John confessed, "I Honestly Love You." The Doors just said, "Hello, I Love You" and Justin Bieber wanted "Somebody to Love."

The Beatles said, "All You Need is Love" but you "Can't Buy Me Love." Roxette claimed that "It Must Have Been Love" while Robert Palmer was "Addicted to Love." Elvis crooned "Love Me Tender" and claimed to be a hunka hunka "Burning Love."

Ray Charles sang, "I Can't Stop Loving you." But Air Supply admitted they were "All Outta Love." Kenny begged Ruby, "Don't take your love to town."

Tim told Faith, "It's Your Love," while Taylor wrote "A Love Story." Dolly wrote it and Whitney sang it, "I Will Always Love You." Jackie DeShannon said it best when she sang that love was "What the World Needs Now" and Haddaway summed it up by asking, "What Is Love?"

Good question. What is love? Let's answer that question with three life-changing truths from the Bible.

LOVE IS THE FIRST FRUIT THAT PRODUCES THE OTHER FRUIT

There are four kinds of love: sexual, affection, friendship, and sacrificial. One of the problems in the English language is that we only have one word for love. We have to use the same word when we say we love God, our sweetheart, and hot dogs. Because we're restricted to the one English word, love can easily be misunderstood.

In contrast, the New Testament was written in Koine Greek, one of the most expressive languages in the world. In this language there are four different Greek words for love. If you want to dig more deeply into these four words, C.S. Lewis has written an amazing book called *The Four Loves* and I recommend it. Let's look at these four loves and see if we can get closer to understanding more about love.

Eros is sensual, sexual attraction

Our English word "erotic" comes from the root of this word. It's not just a sexual love, however. It also includes romantic love. This is the feeling of love people describe when they talk about love at first sight. This love is usually based on physical attraction and it comes and goes. *Eros* never appears in the New Testament.

A man was proposing to his girlfriend and said, "Sweetheart, I want you to marry me. I know I don't have a new car like Johnny Green, or a nice house like Johnny Green. I don't have a lot of money and I'm not handsome like Johnny Green, but I love you and I want you to marry me." She said coyly, "I love you too, but tell me more about this Johnny Green." That's *eros* attraction—it's powerful but it focuses on external things and doesn't go very far down the road.

Storge is family affection

This word describes the love we have for our parents and children. We can choose our friends, but we can't choose our family. We may not like all our family members, but since blood is thicker than water, we show up at family events because of *storge*. When I say, "I love America" I'm referred to this kind of love of country as well. This word doesn't appear in the New Testament either.

Phileo is friendship love

The city of Philadelphia is the city of brotherly love because it is a combination of *phileo* and *adelphos*, which means "brother." This is a powerful love and Aristotle said it was the highest kind of love. This is the kind of love they mean when men say to a buddy, "I love you, man!" or women tell their girlfriends, "I love you like a sister!"

I was browsing through the greeting card section of a store recently and I came across a card in the love section that made me laugh. It read, "If I had an ice-cream cone, I'd give you half. If I had six pieces of candy, I'd give you three. If I had two apples, one would be yours. If I won the lottery...I'd send you a post card from Tahiti." That's a friendship with limits! *Phileo* appears often in the New Testament as "brotherly love."

Agape is sacrificial love

This is the highest and the greatest love, and it is the love mentioned most in the Bible, including the fruit of the Spirit. Jesus said, "Greater love (*agape*) has no one than this, that he lay down his life for his friends." (John 15:13)

C.S. Lewis says all four of these loves blend together, and it is difficult to split them up. But he groups the first three kinds of loves as "need-loves." We all need to be loved in those ways. But he called *agape*, "gift-love." *Agape* is such a special form of love that when the King James translators were looking for a word to use in 1 Corinthians 13, they used the word charity. The word *agape* was rare in Greek literature until the New Testament was written. It was only when Jesus came on the scene that the world first understood the real meaning of this kind of self-sacrificing love. John 3:16 says, "God so loved the world (*agape*) that He gave His one and only Son."

The New Testament scholar William Barclay writes: "*Agape* is a feeling of the mind as much as of the heart; it concerns the will as much as the emotions. It describes the deliberate effort, which we can make only with the power of God, never to seek anything but the best even for those who seek the worst for us."

Agape love is the primary and most important fruit, because it produces all the others. You can't have joy, peace, or patience without first having love. In his letter to the Colossians, Paul switched his metaphors from fruit to clothing. We're challenged to take off the old dirty clothes of the sinful nature and clothe ourselves in the nature of Christ.

MEMORIZE THIS

"Clothe yourselves with compassion, kindness, humility, gentleness and patience...And over all these virtues put on love, which binds them all together in perfect unity." (Colossians 3:12, 14)

Pastor Stuart Briscoe tells the story of a teenager who, unbeknownst to his parents, used to climb down an old fruit tree that grew near his bedroom window. He used it to escape at night and hang out with his friends. One day his dad announced that he was going to cut down the tree because it hadn't produced fruit in several seasons. The kid didn't want to lose his escape route, so when his dad was gone, he and his friends bought a bushel of apples and carefully tied the apples to the branches. When the dad returned, his son said, "Look, Dad, it's a miracle! This tree is now growing apples!" His father smiled and said, "Son, that really *is* a miracle, because that's a pear tree!"

We don't produce the fruit of love by artificially trying to fake our love for other people. Fruit is the outward expression of the inner work that Jesus is accomplishing inside of us. There are several truths I've learned through my study of God's Word about this kind of amazing love.

YOU CAN'T LOVE OTHERS UNTIL YOU REALIZE HOW VERY MUCH GOD LOVES YOU

The only way you can pass on the love of God is to know how deeply God loves you. Do you realize that you are deeply loved by the Creator of the Universe? You may know it in your head, but do you know it in your heart?

The Apostle John wrote his first letter to young Christians to help them grow into maturity. The theme of the entire letter is love. He wrote, "How great is the love the Father has lavished on us, that we should be called children of God! And that is what we are!" (1 John 3:1) What comes to your mind when you think of God lavishing His love on you? He's not just passing it out a little bit at a time—it's not a drip from a faucet but rather an entire flood of His love.

I once read about a woman who grew up on the Great Plains during the Depression, living all her life in poverty. As she was getting older and approaching the age to die, she confessed to her grandchildren that she had always wanted to see the ocean. So they bundled her up in a car and drove three days from the middle of America to the Pacific Ocean. The family walked with her to a bluff overlooking the vast sea, and as she looked at the expanse before her she began to cry. Her family was alarmed and asked her what was wrong. "Are you sad that you've never seen it before?" they wanted to know. As the tears trickled down her face, she smiled and said, "No. I'm just happy to finally see something that God made plenty of!"

I love to stand on the seashore and imagine the vastness of God's love. I love to look up at the starry sky and imagine that God's love is bigger and stronger than the physical universe itself. Paul's prayer for the Christians in Ephesus was that they would "grasp how wide and long and high and deep is the love of Christ, and to know this love that surpasses knowledge." (Ephesians 3:18–19)

Earlier I mentioned some of the songs that have love in the title. The very best love songs are ones that we sing in church. Songs like, "Jesus Loves Me," "Love Lifted Me." "O Love that Will Not Let Me Go" and David Crowder's, "How He Loves."

But of all these songs about God's love, my favorite lyrics come from a song written in 1915 by a Nazarene pastor named Frederick Lehman. The third stanza is adapted from a Jewish poem that is over 1,000 old. To appreciate the meaning, you must remember that this hymn was written at a time when scribes had to use quills, long feathers, with the tips dipped in bottles of ink to write words on parchment. The third verse says:

Could we with ink; the oceans fill;
And were the skies of parchment made;
Were every stalk on earth a quill;
And every man a scribe by trade.
To write the love of God above,
Would drain the oceans dry.
Nor could the scroll contain the whole
Though stretched from sky to sky.

Let me translate that for you. Fill up all the seven seas of the world with ink—trillions and trillions of gallons. Then stretch a roll of paper from one side of the universe to the other side. Take every stick and tree branch on earth and fashion it into a pen. Then give everyone on earth, all seven-plus billion people, one of those pens and have them write about God's love. They would drain the oceans and fill up the sky, but still it wouldn't be enough to cover even a tiny fraction of how much God loves you!

THE ONLY WAY TO LOVE OTHERS IS TO LET JESUS LOVE THEM THROUGH YOU

An old pastor preached one Sunday on love and how this world needs more of it. The next day he had concrete poured for a patio he was building behind his house. Before the concrete set, some neighborhood kids decided to play in it. They took sticks and drew their names in the concrete and left their handprints. When the preacher saw what they did to his patio he was livid. He ran out the back door and screamed, "You kids get outta here!"

The kids ran off and when he walked back inside his wife said,

"Honey, I thought you preached a sermon yesterday on loving everybody. You didn't show much love to those kids, now did you?" He retorted, "Well, what I meant was that I love people in the abstract. I don't love them in the concrete." That's the problem with a lot of people. They say they love people in a non-committal, grand sort of way. But when it comes to loving someone who irritates us, we make exceptions. It's like Linus once said to Lucy in a *Peanuts* cartoon, "I love humanity. It's people I can't stand."

John wrote: "Dear friends, let us love one another, for love comes from God...No one has ever seen God; but if we love one another, God lives in us and his love is made complete in us. We know that we live in him and he in us, because he has given us of his Spirit." (1 John 4:7,12–14)

Lee Ezell wrote in his book, *Porcupine People: Learning to Love the Unlovable*, "Love is an unconditional commitment to an imperfect person. That perfectly describes God's love for us; an unconditional commitment on His part, to us, the imperfect person."

I used to say that some people were unlovable, but someone corrected me. They reminded me that no person is truly unlovable because God loves them. That's correct, so now I just say that some people are unlovely. But Jesus can love unlovely people through you. Do you believe that?

He loves that annoying person so much that He died for him or her. You can't love this unlovely person, so you must rely on Him to do the loving. Ask Jesus to use your smile, eyes, words, and even your hands to show your love. Remember, an apple growing on a tree identifies that tree as an apple tree. When you love unlovely people, you are identifying yourself as a follower of Jesus!

The night before Jesus was crucified; He was at the Passover meal with His disciples. The job of washing feet always fell to the lowliest slave. The disciples were so full of their self-importance that not one of them would stoop to washing feet. So Jesus got up and played the role of a slave. He washed all their feet, even the feet of a disciple named Judas Iscariot. As Jesus washed Judas' feet, He knew is betrayer had already sold Him out for 30 pieces of silver. Yet Jesus loved him enough to humble Himself and lovingly wash his feet. I don't think Jesus gave him the express wash job either. I believe Jesus did an especially thorough job of cleaning around the toenails and between the toes of that man whose feet would later lead the mob to arrest Jesus. If Jesus loved Judas and washed his feet, don't you think He can and will love all kinds of people through you?

During WWII an American soldier died in combat in France, and his two friends desperately wanted to give him a decent burial. They found a cemetery in a nearby village, but it happened to belong to a Roman Catholic church and their friend was Protestant. When they found the priest in charge of the burial grounds, they requested permission to bury their friend. But the priest refused to do so because the man wasn't a Catholic. When the priest saw their disappointment, he had a change of heart and explained that they could bury their friend immediately outside the fence, which they did.

They later returned that week to visit the grave outside the fence but couldn't find it. Their search led them back to the priest and they asked him what had happened to the grave of their friend. The priest sighed a deep, knowing sigh and told them a story. During the night after their visit, the priest was unable to sleep. He kept seeing the faces of that dead man's friends and their desperate desire to honor their comrade. Finally, when he realized sleep would not come until he took action, he got up from bed. He went to the garage and with shovel in hand went to the cemetery guided only by the moonlight. At once the priest began digging around the fence until he was able to move it several feet to encircle the freshly dug grave of the man. Satisfied, the priest returned home to bed and slept soundly.

Sometimes people put themselves outside the fence of your love because of their behavior. Is there someone you need to move your personal boundaries to include in your circle of love, even if they've shut you out?

TAKEAWAY TRUTH

Put What You're Learning Into Practice

I want you to envision the face of the person you have the hardest time loving. This person gets on your nerves and when you see them walking your way your first thought is, "Oh no." The person may be a family member, a friend of a friend, a fellow church member, or someone you work with. It might even be your boss.

Almost every day you're going to be confronted with people who are unlovely. Will you make a choice that you're going to love them the way God loves you? Don't try to do it in your own strength. Just whisper a quick prayer, "Jesus, help me love this person." You may have to repeat this prayer several times a day.

CHAPTER 3

Joy Is A Choice—
Not A Feeling

As we examine the fruit of the Spirit, we should remember the maxim: Fruit is the outward expression of the inward nature. When you see a plum hanging on a tree, you can say, "That's a plum tree." When you see these nine personality traits displayed in the life of a Christian, you can say, "There's a Spirit-filled Christian."

In this chapter, we're going to examine the fruit of joy. I've always loved the word *joy* and the name *Joy*. In fact, my very first girlfriend was named Joy Thompson. I was in the third grade and Joy was Little Miss Peanut at the Peanut Festival in Dothan, Alabama. My only trouble was that one of my friends named Alan Silverman liked Joy too. There were only two Jewish families in Florala, and Alan's family was one of them. We competed for Joy's attention, and she seemed to enjoy it. I'll never forget the day that Alan took me aside and said, "David, my mother said that I have to marry a Jewish girl, and Joy isn't Jewish, so I guess you can have her." I didn't understand much of the Bible then, but that was the first time I said, "Thank God for the Jews!"

But joy is more than a name. It's a powerful, positive reaction that we display when we're filled with the Holy Spirit. As followers of Jesus Christ, we have something so rich and valuable that everyone in the world is looking for it.

Years ago some archaeologists were excavating the ruins of the Mamertine prison in Rome and found something inspiring. Thousands of Christians were imprisoned there before they were sent to the Coliseum to fight wild animals and to die as martyrs. The archeologists found a fragment of a letter among the ruins. It was written during the third century, during the most intense time of persecution against Christians. We don't know who wrote it, but the message of this letter is unforgettable: "It's a bad world, an incredibly bad world. But I have discovered in the midst of it a quiet and holy people who have learned a great secret. They have found a joy which is a thousand times better than the pleasure of our sinful life. They are despised and persecuted, but they care not. They have overcome the world. These people are the Christians—and I am one of them."

It is a bad world—an incredibly bad world. But God offers to fill you with His joy. All these gifts of the Spirit are grace-gifts, but of all the nine virtues, joy is the closest to grace. Grace and joy are twins, not identical, but born from the same root word. The Greek word for *grace* is *karis* and the word for joy is *kara*. You might say that joy is grace enjoyed. In this chapter we will explore the meaning of joy, where to find joy, and how to express joy.

JOY IS A CHEERFUL ATTITUDE IN EVERY CIRCUMSTANCE OF LIFE

Some confused souls believe it is the role of our federal government to make us happy and keep us happy. Our Declaration of Independence does mention three inalienable rights given to us. But these are given to us by our Creator, NOT by our government. And contrary to what some people assume, these three rights aren't life, liberty, and happiness. The wording of the Constitution says that they are life, liberty, and the PURSUIT of happiness.

And pursue it we do! Americans devote much of their time and energy trying to find happiness. Many surveys have asked Americans, "What is it that you most want in life?" And the overwhelming majority of Americans answer: "I want to be happy." Then the survey often follows up with this question, "What would it take to make you happy?" The top answer to the second question is, "I don't know." That's very revealing about our culture today.

What people don't realize is that they need JOY not happiness. Happiness comes from the word *hap*, which means *luck* or *happenings*. Happiness rises and falls with what happens in your life, but joy remains constant regardless of circumstances. Joy is an inner attitude of cheer that manifests itself through outward celebration.

Joy is an important word in the Bible. It appears 158 times, and "rejoice" appears another 198 times. In the Old Testament there are 27 different colorful words to describe joy. Some of the basic meanings are to "run around with delight" and "to shine like the brightness of the sun."

When missionaries to the Eskimos in Northern Alaska were trying to translate the Bible into one of their dialects, they discovered there was no Eskimo word for "joy." So the missionaries looked to see what the most delightful experience in the village was. They observed that the happiest, most joyful moments were in the evenings when they fed their sled dogs. The dogs would leap, wag their tails, and yelp for joy—the kind of dog antics that made the Eskimos smile as well. The missionaries decided to use that scene to translate the word *joy*. Think about this when you read the passage from Luke where it says, "After the resurrection, the disciples saw Jesus and were *full of joy*." For the Eskimos, it would read, "When the disciples saw Jesus, they wagged their tails with delight." That's true joy.

No, joy isn't happiness. It's so much more! Bill Bright, the founder of Campus Crusade, wrote: "Joy is like the sun, always shining even when night falls or clouds cover it. Happiness is like the moon, waxing and waning. Happiness is born in the mind; joy in the heart. Happiness comes from humans; joy comes only from God." Dr. Adrian Rogers, another spiritual giant in my life, wrote about the difference this way: "Happiness is like cosmetics; joy is like character. Happiness comes from outside circumstances; joy comes from within. Happiness meets surface needs; joy meets your deepest needs. In times of suffering, happiness usually evaporates and disappears; but joy often intensifies in times of suffering."

In fact, the best time to check your joy level isn't when things are going great in your life. It's when things are lousy. It's easy to have joy when you feel good, when everyone loves you, and all your bills are being paid. But can you still rejoice when your world crumbles in?

MEMORIZE THIS

"Consider it pure joy, my brothers, whenever you face trials of many kinds, because you know that the testing of your faith develops perseverance." (James 1:2-3)

Joy becomes more valuable when you find it at the darkest, most depressing times of your life. I love the story found in Acts 16 where Paul and Silas had been arrested, beaten, and thrown in prison for sharing the Gospel. The only stocks and bonds they knew weren't from Wall Street; they were actual wooden stocks around their necks and iron bonds on their hands and feet.

Picture Paul and Silas with bleeding backs, kneeling side-by-side with their heads in those wooden stocks. Did they complain about their rights and demand that justice be done? No, they decided to display their joy. The Bible says that at midnight they started praying and singing songs to God. They didn't allow their circumstance to control them; they chose to control their circumstance. Despite their suffering, they started rejoicing in God. I don't know what songs they sang, but early Christians often sang parts of the Old Testament. They might have been singing the words from Nehemiah 8:10, "The Joy of the Lord is my strength..."

Maybe God started tapping His toe along with the music and when God taps His toe, things happen. The Bible says there was an earthquake that shook that prison. Nobody was killed, but the stocks burst open and the chains fell away. Joy had won the day. The jailer, who was responsible for the prisoners, prepared to fall on his sword and kill himself for losing those in his charge. But Paul assured him,

"We're all here and accounted for!" The jailer then realized there was something to the message of the Gospel that these men had been sharing. He asked them, "Sirs, what must I do to be saved?" Paul said, "Believe on the Lord Jesus Christ and you will be saved." He did, and that night the same man who had bloodied their backs washed their wounds and found the joy of the Lord himself.

JOY IS A CHOICE TO ALLOW JESUS TO CONTROL YOUR PERSONALITY

Joy isn't a feeling. It's a choice. Our joy comes from Jesus, and the extent to which you surrender your personality to His, the more you will experience His joy. It's not MY joy that is valuable. I can only do so much in my own strength. Rather, it's having the joy of Jesus that gets us through life's toughest storms. Jesus said, "I have told you these things so that you will be filled with my joy. Yes, your joy will overflow!" (John 15:11 NLT) If you're looking for more joy in your life, focus on Jesus. He is the source of all true joy. C.S. Lewis said it well: "It is not so much the joy of the Lord we are seeking as the Lord of Joy Himself."

When I was very young we would visit my great aunt Nellie who lived in the Florida Panhandle. Aunt Nellie didn't have any running water in the house, just an old well. Sometimes the responsibility of filling up a bucket with well water for the day's chores fell to me. I'd drop the bucket attached to a rope into the dark depths of that old well and guess when I thought the bucket was full so I could pull it back up to the surface. But I never got a full bucket of water. Aunt Nellie went with me once and taught me how to fill up the bucket properly. She said, "David, the only way you can tell when the bucket is full is when you hear it overflowing." That worked. I'd listen to hear if water was overflowing the bucket, and that's how I knew it was full.

That's the same way you can know that your life is full of Jesus. When you are full of His joy it will overflow to others. One of the meanings of the word *joy* is shining and brightness. When Moses spent time with God on Mt. Sinai, he came back to the Hebrew people and they noticed there was a supernatural glow about his face. He couldn't hide the fact that He had been with God. The best way to express the joy of Jesus is to spend time with Him.

When you're full of the joy of the Lord, it's hard to keep it secret. People can see it in your face. There's a story from the days of California Gold Rush about three prospectors who found a rich gold vein on the property they were mining. They were thrilled, but they were also afraid that when word got around, the other miners would crowd them out before they could file a claim. So, they all three took a vow of silence about this discovery.

When they traveled into town to file the claim and to buy more equipment, true to their vow, they didn't say one word about the gold. After they loaded up the equipment they started back to the mine, but by then a crowd of people was following them. Perplexed, they stopped and asked why the people were trailing behind them. They found out that they didn't have to say anything about gold. Others could see in their faces that they had found something very valuable. That's a great testimony of a Christian. Our faces should be aglow with the overflow of the joy of the Lord.

I've always loved airplanes. When I was in seminary, I worked at a general aviation fixed base operator, fueling the aircraft and parking them in the hangars. I would sometimes help the mechanics repair the engines. One day, one of the older mechanics stopped working and said to me. "I just need to know what's different about you. You seem to be happy all the time. What is it?"

What he called happiness, I call the joy of the Lord. As we were changing out the spark plugs in that airplane engine, I was able to tell him about the difference Jesus had made in my life.

Is the joy of Jesus overflowing in your life so that people can see a difference? That's what joy is, and in maintaining a close relationship with Jesus is where you'll find it. But is it realistic to find ways to express your joy every day? That's what we'll look at next.

JOY IS EXPRESSED BY TRUE GENEROSITY

The best expression of joy isn't in a having a constantly shining face or dancing around with delight. The best expression of it is an unselfish attitude of giving. The Bible says, "Remember the words the Lord Jesus himself said: 'It is more blessed [that's the word *makarion* that means a joyful life] to give than to receive.'" (Acts 20:35) A joyful person is a generous person and vice versa. Giving involves so much more than giving financially. Here are four ways to express the joy of Jesus in your everyday life.

Give thanks in every situation

Joyful people develop an attitude of gratitude. Sour people are grumbly hateful, but joyous people are humbly grateful. The Bible says, "Be joyful always; pray continually; give thanks in all circumstances, for this is God's will for you in Christ Jesus." (1 Thessalonians 5:16–18)

Give away your material possessions

The Bible says, "God loves a cheerful giver." The word *cheerful* comes from the word *hilaron*. It's our word hilarious. God loves hilarious givers. In His parable about the sower Jesus spoke about some people who have the seed of God's Word planted in their hearts, but the worries of this world and possessions choke out the good seed. The biggest sin among Christians today is the sin of hoarding and materialism. We accumulate more and more stuff and then we worry that someone may take our stuff, or that someone might have better stuff. Materialism and greed destroy joy. Generosity feeds your joy.

J. L. Kraft founded the Kraft Foods company and was a committed Christian. He came to the point where he was consistently giving away 25% of his wealth. He said, "The only investment I ever made which has paid consistently increasing dividends is the money I have given to the Lord."

Give yourself in serving others

When I was a college student I first encountered the acrostic for the letters J.O.Y. They stand for, "Jesus first; Others second; Yourself last." That's a good formula for joy. Our model and source of joy is Jesus. The Bible says, "Let us fix our eyes on Jesus, the author and perfecter of our faith, who for the joy set before him endured the cross, scorning its shame, and sat down at the right hand of the throne of God." (Hebrews 12:2) Did you catch that phrase, "who for the JOY set before him, endured the cross?" He didn't see joy IN the cross; He saw the joy PAST the cross in the resurrection and ascension. Joy gives us the ability to look through the tough times of life to the reward God offers on the other side of it.

Give hope to those who need it

The most joyous people I know are also those who share their faith on a regular basis. In fact, whenever Christians talk to me about how they've lost the joy of their salvation, my first question is this: "When was the last time you shared your faith with someone?" When you don't share the good news with people that Jesus loves them and can save them, then you become spiritually introverted. You can become stale and sour.

Do you know what creates JOY in heaven? It's not when 5,000 well-dressed Christians gather in church to sing praises to God. It's not when we give a million dollars to feed the hungry. The one thing that creates joy in heaven is when one person turns from their sins and puts their faith in Jesus. Jesus said, "There is rejoicing in the presence of the angels of God over one sinner who repents." (Luke 15:10)

Joy is a choice, not an emotion, but you can use your joy to "faith" (not fake) your way into the emotion of cheerfulness. You can choose to exchange your spirit of sadness for a garment of praise. According to Isaiah 61:3, God makes this promise to give all those who mourn "beauty instead of ashes, the oil of joy instead of mourning, and a garment of praise instead of a spirit of despair." When you wake up every morning, you have a choice. You can wallow in the ashes of the world, or you can choose the beauty that God offers. You can give in to mourning, or you can have the oil of joy covering you. Are you burdened down with a spirit of heaviness? You can choose to praise God regardless of how you feel. Joy is a choice!

To be joyful isn't just a good choice; it's a command from God. First Thessalonians 5:16 says, "Be joyful always." In Philippians 4:4 Paul wrote, "Rejoice in the Lord, always. I will say it again: Rejoice!" He was in prison when he wrote that. He didn't say, "Rejoice in your prison" he said, "Rejoice in the Lord." The Bible never says, "Rejoice in your bank account." Or "Rejoice in your house." If those things are your source of joy, when they're taken away, your joy goes away with them. The Bible doesn't say, "Rejoice in your good health." Or "Rejoice in your sharp mind." You could lose your health or mental acuity in a moment, and where would your joy be? You'll never find anything in the Bible that says, "Rejoice in your big screen TV." Or "Rejoice in your computer." Or "Rejoice in your car." All of those things are temporary and will someday be gone. But if you're rejoicing in the Lord, your source of joy will exist long past the world as we know it.

Pastor Adrian Rogers once told a story about how a member of his church came to understand the meaning and power of real joy. This lady wrote him a letter recounting her experience. One morning as she was preparing to go to work, she was listening to a recording of Adrian's message about joy and the Holy Spirit used his words to convict her. Adrian preached, "What is the source of your joy? If a tragic or traumatic thing happens—a child dies, your car is stolen, your home burglarized, valuable possessions lost—and you lose your joy, then you might well consider where your joy comes from. If your joy is in things—or even a person—and you lose that, you can lose your joy. But, if your joy comes from the Lord, and He is enthroned in your heart, that joy cannot be taken away."

She was still meditating on that message when she got into her car to drive to work. She turned on the Christian radio station she typically listened to, and Steve Green was singing a song entitled, "That's Where the Joy Comes From." She was amazed at how the words of that song supported what she had just heard Adrian say.

Let's pick up the rest of the story from the letter she wrote to

Adrian: "Soon after I arrived at work, one of my sons called to tell me that when he drove to our house about 10 a.m., he found all of the doors open, and the house terribly ransacked, and quite a lot of our belongings stolen. Right then, I realized that the Lord had been preparing me for this that very morning. I thought of the words of the song, and what you had said in your message, that came so clearly to my mind. If I ever wondered what it's like when God speaks to a person, I know now.

"When I got home, I saw the awful sight. I never even felt like shedding a tear. It took us all afternoon to straighten up the mess the burglars left. And yet, this feeling of joy kept popping out. I want you to know that day is a day I will never forget—not because of the burglary, but because of the way that God spoke to me and prepared me through your message...I really saw today that Jesus alone is the source of my joy. Now I know firsthand that thieves may rob my treasures, but they don't hold the key that leads into the sanctuary where God's Spirit lives in me."

How's your joy today? If Jesus is the source of your joy, your joy will be the same yesterday, today, and forevermore because Jesus is the same yesterday, today, and forevermore!

TAKEAWAY TRUTH
Put What You're Learning Into Practice

Psychologists say that gratitude is the healthiest emotion. Have you noticed the most joyous people are the ones who are the most thankful? Take a moment this week and make a list of blessings for which you need to thank God.

Write a personal note or email to two people who have blessed you and thank them. The more thankful you are, the more joyful you'll become.

CHAPTER 4

Peace In A World Of Pressure

World peace is a noble goal, and it's always a good answer in a beauty contest. But according to an article in *The New York Times*, out of almost 4,000 years of recorded human history, there have only been about 200 years of peace—and those years of peace are just pauses for the armies to reload!

Ron Artest, a forward for the LA Lakers, was known as one of the most aggressive and violent players in the NBA. Hoping to change his reputation, in 2011 he legally changed his name to Metta World Peace. That didn't change his behavior though. Just a few months after he changed his name, he was ejected from a game for violently elbowing James Harden in the face. You can call yourself what you want, but unless you have Jesus in your heart, you'll never find inner peace.

Is it possible to have true inner peace? I found a quote where a woman wrote: "My therapist told me the way to achieve true inner peace is to finish what I start. So far today, I have finished two bags of chips and a chocolate cake. I feel better already."

A man was leaving church one Sunday and said to his pastor, "Your message today reminded me of the peace and mercy of God." The pastor said, "Why, thank you." The man said, "Don't thank me. It was like the peace of God because it passed all understanding, and it was like the mercy of God because it seemed to endure forever!"

Some people think peace is the absence of problems, but it's not possible to go through life without trouble and adversity. Job said, "Man is born to trouble as surely as sparks fly upward." (Job 5:7) Let's start with a working definition of peace. **"Peace is not the absence of problems. Peace is God's gift of serenity in the midst of your problems."**

We've all known people who crumbled under the pressures of life. That would be the reaction of most people, in fact. But we've also known people who are going through the most painful and difficult trials life could hand them, yet they never seem to lose their peace. They never lose their sense of spiritual equilibrium. These are people who have discovered what it is to have the spiritual fruit of peace. It's not *their* peace. It's the peace of Jesus, God's gift of serenity, abiding in their personality.

In the early days of the church in Jerusalem, Peter was arrested and thrown in prison. He was scheduled to be executed the next day. The Bible explains, "That's when King Herod got it into his head to go after some of the church members. He murdered James, John's brother. When he saw how much it raised his popularity ratings with the Jews, he arrested Peter—and had him thrown in jail, putting four squads of four soldiers each to guard him. He was probably planning a public lynching after Passover. That night, even though shackled to two soldiers, one on either side, Peter slept like a baby." (Acts 12:1–6 *The Message*)

This wasn't the King Herod who was alive when Jesus was born; this was his grandson Herod Agrippa. But like his grandfather, he was also a cruel and violent man. After having James beheaded, he arrested the ringleader Peter and threw him in prison, probably the notorious Roman Citadel. He put him in chains, surrounded by 16 soldiers, in a place that was like being on death row in a maximum-security wing of a prison. How would we respond if we knew we were going to die by execution in the morning? For most of us it would have been an episode of *Sleepless in the Citadel*. But Peter slept like a baby—now THAT'S inner peace!

The question that begs our attention from this incident is HOW could Peter possess the kind of personal peace and serenity that allowed him to SLEEP at a time like this? Simple. He knew some foundational truths about God that allowed his heart to be filled with serenity. Did Peter know something we don't know? Actually, anyone can find peace in the midst of trouble if they embrace the following three truths about God.

KNOW THAT GOD IS THERE...HE SEES WHAT YOU'RE FACING

Peter realized God was with him there in the prison, and I'm sure he prayed before he went to sleep. Before the cross, in the Garden of Gethsemane, Peter slept when he should have been praying. But now after the resurrection and the coming of the Holy Spirit, he slept *because* he prayed. When you face hard times, the first thing to do is pray, and the last thing to do is trust God. When you talk to God, you shouldn't think that He's a million miles away in heaven. He's right there wherever you are. He sees what you're facing.

Corrie Ten Boom, who survived the atrocities of a Nazi prison camp said: "There is no pit so deep that God is not deeper still." So when you find yourself facing a situation that would threaten to rob you of sleep, remember this powerful promise from God's Word. "Don't worry about anything; instead, pray about everything. Tell God what you need, and thank him for all he has done. Then you will experience God's peace, which exceeds anything we can understand. His peace will guard your hearts and minds as you live in Christ Jesus." (Philippians 4:6–7 NLT)

Peter had something much more powerful than soldiers guarding his heart—it was the peace of God that passes understanding. And he had that peace because he refused to worry. Instead, he prayed and then he slept.

He wasn't the only one praying, of course. The Bible says the church was praying for Peter to be released. To me, what happened next is rather funny. In the middle of the night God sent an angel to rescue Peter who was sleeping so soundly that the angel had to poke him in the ribs to wake him up. He saw that the chains around his

feet and hands had fallen off, but Peter was so sleepy that the angel
had to tell him step by step what to do next. He said, "Put on your
clothes, now put on your coat, now follow me..." They walked right
out of the prison and the guards never saw them—it was as if they
were invisible. When Peter hit the streets and arrived at the house
where the prayer meeting was going on, he knocked on the door.

A young girl named Rhoda answered and couldn't believe her
eyes. She was so surprised that she just left Peter standing in the
street! She ran to the group and announced, "Peter's here!" Only
they didn't believe her. I imagine they may have scoffed and said,
"That's impossible. He's in prison and we're praying for his release.
So don't bother us! We've got to pray!" Obviously, they didn't have
much faith in what they were asking God to do. But it doesn't take a
lot of faith for God to move mountains—or open prison doors—or
to give you a peace that passes human understanding.

When you're going through the fire, you should pray and ask
God to give you the kind of peace Peter had. You may be familiar
with a famous prayer called "The Serenity Prayer" that many 12-step
programs use. The classic form that you often read goes like this:
"God, grant me the serenity to accept the things I cannot change,
the courage to change the things I can, and the wisdom to know the
difference." That's a great prayer. Someone created a parody called
"The Senility Prayer" which reads: "God, grant me the senility to
forget the people I never liked anyway, the good fortune to run into
the ones I do, and the eyesight to know the difference!"

Let me give you the full story about the real Serenity Prayer. An
American pastor and theologian, Reinhold Niebuhr, first wrote it.
Dr. Niebuhr was born in Missouri in the late 1880s. His parents were

German immigrants and he published this prayer in German, his first language. Here is the actual translation of it:

"God, give us grace to accept with serenity the things that cannot be changed; Courage to change the things which should be changed; And the Wisdom to distinguish the one from the other. Living one day at a time; Enjoying one moment at a time; Accepting hardship as a pathway to peace; Taking, as Jesus did, this sinful world as it is, not as I would have it; Trusting that You will make all things right, if I surrender to Your will; So that I may be reasonably happy in this life and supremely happy with You forever in the next. Amen."

So when you're in pain, searching for peace, the first thing to know is that God is there—and He sees what you're facing. Our American founders used a word for God that we don't use much anymore. It is a word that so describes God's character that our Founding Fathers capitalized it and substituted it for God. It appears in our Declaration of Independence.

It is such a powerful word for God that the Baptist preacher Roger Williams gave it as the name of a city that is now the capital of our smallest state. It's the word PROVIDENCE. *Pro* means "ahead." *Videre* means, "to see." We get our word "video" from it. When used as a title of God, it means that God not only sees what's happening to us NOW, He sees what's ahead. No matter what you're going through right now, God has already seen the video of what's going to happen. And trust me, it's all working together, somehow and someway, for your GOOD. Better yet, trust the Word of God that teaches us that very truth in Romans 8:28, that says: "We know that all things work together for the good of those who love God, who are called according to his purpose."

Sadly, there are a lot of Christians who are spending sleepless nights worrying because they have forgotten that God is there with them. There's a line from one of my favorite hymns, *What a Friend We Have in Jesus*, that talks about the needless suffering we go through when we don't take things to God in prayer.

KNOW THAT GOD IS AWARE...HE KNOWS WHAT YOU'RE FEARING

Can you sleep like a baby even when you are afraid of what might happen tomorrow? In January 2005 the Oklahoma Sooners lost the national championship football game to USC in the Orange Bowl. I confess that I am an Oklahoma fan, so I must add the footnote that USC had an ineligible player and later forfeited the game and the title. Still, OU lost badly—they were trounced 55–19. At the press conference the next morning Coach Bob Stoops was asked how he slept after the game. He responded that he slept like a baby. Then he said, "I'd sleep a few minutes, wake up and cry, then sleep a few more minutes and wake up and cry again."

Peter could sleep soundly because he claimed the promise of God found in Psalm 4:8, "I will lie down and sleep in peace, for you alone, O Lord, make me dwell in safety." God is aware of every aspect of your life. In Psalm 139 we learn that God says He knows everything about us. He knows what we're going to say before we say it. He is aware of every situation we're going through in life.

I also love the promise of Psalm 121:4, which says, "He who watches over Israel will neither slumber nor sleep." You can substitute your name there and say, "He who watches over _____ neither slumbers nor sleeps." How do I know this is true? The very next verse,

Psalm 121:5 says, "The Lord watches over YOU." God doesn't get tired, so He doesn't need sleep. And since He's watching over you all night, you might as well go to sleep instead of worrying about tomorrow.

Do you have trouble sleeping at night? Over 70 million Americans suffer from some form of insomnia. Women are more likely as men to struggle with sleep deficit than men. Some of you ladies may say that's because there's not much going on in men's brains to start with. But we worry, too, sometimes.

Someone said the human brain is an amazing instrument. It starts working the moment you're born and doesn't stop until you stand up in front of a crowd to speak! Actually, your brain never stops its activity. And that's one of the reasons why people have trouble sleeping at night. Their brain just keeps on working, bringing up what happened earlier that day or what might happen tomorrow. That's also why we dream—the brain continuously works without an on/off switch. But wouldn't it be great to have control over our brain like that? At night you could just get into bed and switch off your brain and set it to come back on the next morning!

Unfortunately, you can't switch off your brain, but you CAN change the channel! One of my favorite verses is Isaiah 26:3. In fact, I often include it at the end of an email. It says, "You will keep in perfect peace him whose mind is steadfast, because he trusts in you." When I wake up in the middle of the night, I put my brain on the Jesus channel. I start praying, and I often fall back asleep within a few minutes. Try switching your brain to the Jesus channel the next time you are wide awake in the night.

MEMORIZE THIS

"You will keep in perfect peace him whose mind is steadfast, because he trusts in you." Isaiah 26:3

KNOW THAT GOD CARES...HE SHARES HOW YOU'RE FEELING

Peter could sleep not only because he knew God was there with him and that God was aware of His situation, but he also knew that God cared. Jesus had been in the same Citadel where he was imprisoned just a few weeks earlier. He had been beaten and tortured by Roman soldiers—perhaps even some of the same ones guarding Peter.

The writer of Hebrews says that Jesus, our High Priest, knows our weaknesses. He was tempted in every way we are tempted, yet He never sinned. Worry is a sin, and we know Jesus was *tempted* to worry. Fear is a sin, and we know Jesus was *tempted* to be afraid. Jesus knows EXACTLY how you're feeling when you are afraid. He shares the feelings of our weaknesses. More important, in our weakest times, God cares for you.

Once Jesus and the disciples were in a storm on the Sea of Galilee. They cried out, "Don't you care if we drown?" (Mark 4:38) That's a good question. If you're honest, you might admit that you've wanted to ask God the same thing. *"God, I'm hurting, don't you care?" "God, I've lost my job, don't you care?" "God, I've got cancer, don't you care?" "God, I'm all alone, don't you care?"*

He DOES care. Sometimes Jesus calms the storms of life, but most often He calms our hearts. We all know that a hurricane is a devastating force of nature. But at the center of every hurricane there's an "eye" where it's calm and peaceful. The sun is shining, the air is still, and even birds fly around in this unique center of calm. Peter was tucked inside the eye of a hurricane that night in prison. When you know that God cares for you, you can be at rest while all around you the storm rages.

Do you recall what Jesus was doing while the storm on the Sea of Galilee was raging? He was sleeping. He's the only One who can sleep in a storm, so the only way we can sleep during the storms of life is to allow Jesus to give us His peace.

How much does God care for you? Listen to His words. "Can a mother forget the baby at her breast and have no compassion on the child she has borne? Though she may forget, I will not forget you! See, I have engraved you on the palms of my hands." (Isaiah 49:15–16) In the original Hebrew it indicates that this is more than just your name inked on His hands. The great British pastor Charles Spurgeon pointed this out: "God says, 'I have engraved YOU.' He didn't say, 'your name.' The name is there, but that is not all. God says, 'I have engraved your person, your image, your circumstances, your sins, your temptations, your weaknesses, your wants, your works, everything about you, all that concerns you; I have put all of this together here.' Will you ever say again that your God has forsaken you when He has engraved you on His own palms?"

We've all known people who take a pen and write something on their hand when they wanted to remember to get milk on the way home or return a call. A pastor friend once told me about a wedding he performed where the bride and groom had written their own vows, and they were going to recite them from memory. The groom was afraid he would forget, so he wrote his vows on the palm of his hand. The only trouble is that grooms are usually nervous, and they sweat a lot. (I never say, "Wilt thou?" to the groom because he's usually already wilted!) When it came time to read his vows, he opened his hand and there was just a blue blob of smeared ink. He was so flustered that when he and the bride saw the mess they both burst into laughter. So he just blurted out, "All I can say is 'I love you!'" That was enough.

When the resurrected Jesus appeared to the disciples on the first Easter Sunday, Thomas was missing. He was skeptical when they reported to him that Jesus was alive. Furthermore, he added, he wouldn't believe unless he could place his fingers in the nail prints in Jesus' hands. A week later, Jesus appeared to Thomas and invited him to do just that. Thomas fell down and confessed, "My Lord, and my God."

Whenever you doubt how much God cares for you, I invite you to do what Thomas did and consider the scars of Jesus. Christ says, "I care for you so much that I took the nails in My hands for you. I have you engraved on My hands."

Since God cares for you, He can give you peace in spite of your pain. I love to tell the true story behind the hymn, It Is Well with My Soul. Horatio Spafford was a wealthy lawyer from Chicago and a Presbyterian elder. He was also a close friend of the evangelist Dwight L. Moody. Spafford's life was filled with tragedy. First, his only son died at age four from scarlet fever. Then, he lost most of his wealth when the Great Chicago Fire wiped out all the real estate he had bought on Lake Michigan. But he refused to become bitter. He scraped together what money he had left and planned to take his wife and four remaining daughters to England to help with an evangelistic crusade that Moody was leading. At the last minute, business kept him in Chicago, so he put his family on the ship bound for England and planned to sail a few days later and join them.

Then the ship his wife and daughters were on collided with another ship and sank. All four of his daughters died, but his wife was rescued. The telegram she sent to her husband simply said, "Saved alone. What shall I do?" And she gave her contact information. Spafford, in shock and disbelief, immediately boarded a ship to join his devastated wife.

Imagine. The man's son has died. He has lost most of his wealth. And now his four daughters have drowned. His story reads like a modern tale of Job. Yet while Spafford was on the ship, gazing out at the rolling waves, he was inspired to write the words to an iconic song. It's in the public domain and has given hope to many of us:

When peace like a river attendeth my way;
When sorrows like sea billows roll.
Whatever my lot, Thou hast taught me to say,
"It is well. It is well with my soul."

How could a man find such peace? Jesus was in him. How could Peter sleep when he faced death? Jesus lived within him by the power of the Holy Spirit. How can you have peace like a river in your soul? You will have it when Jesus lives in you.

Jesus is your source of serenity. He said, "I have told you these things, so that in me you may have peace. In this world you will have trouble. But take heart! I have overcome the world." (John 16:33) Did you notice Jesus didn't say, "WITH ME you'll have peace." He said, "IN ME, you may have peace." When Christ is in you, and you are in Christ, you can have His peace.

TAKEAWAY TRUTH
Put What You're Learning Into Practice

A lady once wrote me saying she had trouble sleeping after her husband died. Then she memorized the twenty-third Psalm and would recite it at night. She would emphasize the personal pronouns and envision the setting as she silently quoted it. I want you to try this exercise this week. When you turn off the light to go to sleep, focus your mind on this psalm. Emphasize the personal pronouns. Envision the tranquil scene. I'll get you started below...

The Lord is MY shepherd, I shall not want.
He makes ME lie down in green pastures,
He leads ME beside the still waters...

CHAPTER 5

I Need Patience Now!

You can tell a lot about a person when they're waiting for an elevator to reach their destination. Some people stand there swaying back and forth watching the progress of the elevator. And sometimes you'll see someone keep punching the up or down button, as if that will make the elevator arrive sooner.

So how patient are you? What is your PQ (Patience Quotient)? Truth be told, we all need more patience. It's important to understand three truths about one of the most difficult character traits to develop: patience.

TRUTH #1: PATIENCE IS THE ABILITY TO ACCEPT DELAY OR DISAPPOINTMENT GRACIOUSLY

I like the story of the kindergarten teacher who lived in the snowbelt. It was the end of a long winter day in class and she was struggling and straining to stuff one her student's feet into his snow boots. When she finally finished the boy casually said, "They're on the wrong feet."

So she worked to get them off and put them on the other feet. That's when the boy said, "These aren't my boots."

By now she was sweating, but she took them off again and was going to look for his boots when the boy explained, "They're my brother's boots, but my mother told me to wear them today." Almost at the breaking limit, she worked to get them back on his feet again.

When she finished, she clapped her hands and said, "Finally! Now, where are your mittens?" Without flinching, the boy then said, "I stuffed them in the toes of my boots."

Our default reaction to the things that try our patience is anger. Life is full of delays and disappointments. Patience is the ability to allow God's grace to control our personality so that we can respond graciously in all circumstances. The Bible teaches that God Himself is patient. The Greek word for patience is *makrothumos*, a combination of two words, *makro*, meaning large or long (in computers we have micros and macros) and *thumos*, which means anger or temper. In other words, patience means having a long fuse on your temper. That's why the King James Version translates the word as long suffering. The Bible says, "The Lord is gracious and compassionate, slow to anger and rich in love." (Psalm 145:8)

The mother of impatience is anger. When you are delayed or disappointed, you want to get angry. But patience is the long fuse God gives you to not lose your cool. Patience is a powerful virtue. Solomon wrote, "Better to be patient than powerful; better to have self-control than to conquer a city." (Proverbs 16:32 NLT)

I heard the personal testimony of a successful business owner who was also a deacon in a Baptist church in Houston, Texas. He explained how he struggled with impatience and anger and told the story about how one morning he got in his car and discovered the battery was dead. He was already frustrated, so he jumped into his wife's car because she was away on a trip. When he got on the expressway there was a traffic jam and the highway became a parking lot. He was seething about being late, and to make matters worse, the guy in the car behind him honked his horn at him. He looked in the mirror and thought, "Doesn't that idiot know I can't go anywhere?" He shook his fist in the air at the guy. But the guy in car behind must have thought he was waving, because he just waved back and honked his horn again.

That's when the businessman snapped. He slammed the car into park, got out, and stomped back to the car behind him. The guy rolled down his window and the man reached in and grabbed him by the collar and said, "Can't you see that I can't go anywhere? If you blow your horn one more time you're going to eat my fist."

The guy in the car was perplexed. He quietly pointed ahead and said, "Man, I was just doing what your bumper sticker said. It says, 'Honk if you love Jesus.'"

The businessman jerked his head around and sure enough, without his knowledge, his wife had added that bumper sticker to her car. He said the Holy Spirit convicted him immediately standing on that highway. He said to the man in the car, "Sir, I do love Jesus. But I sure didn't act like it to you. Will you please forgive me?"

That incident changed his life. He realized that his anger and impatience had threatened his witness. He asked God to give him the strength to be more patient. And he said that whenever anyone honks at him now, he just imagines they've seen a "Honk if you love Jesus" sticker and he smiles and waves.

There's an old Chinese proverb that says, "One moment of patience may ward off great disaster. One moment of impatience may ruin a whole life." How short is your fuse when it comes to frustrating people and exasperating situations?

TRUTH #2: PATIENCE IS RARE BECAUSE IT'S CONTRARY TO OUR NATURE AND OUR CULTURE

It's human nature to be impatient. We aren't naturally wired to be patient. For instance, imagine an infant in a crib. He wakes up in the middle of the night and is hungry. He doesn't lie there and think, "I know Mom and Dad are tired. So I'll just wait until the morning to let them know I need something to eat." Nope. He wants to be fed, and he wants to be fed NOW! Children aren't patient. They don't know the difference between "No" and "Not yet."

Just as there is a direct correlation between immaturity and impatience from a human standpoint, that's also true spiritually. As we mature in Christ, we should become more patient. Is that true in your life?

A mother was driving on a long trip with her four-year-old son. He kept asking repeatedly, "Are we there yet? When are we going to get there? When are we going to get there?" Finally, she was so irritated that she said, "We've got over 100 miles to go, so don't ask me again when we're going to get there." There was silence for a few miles then he asked, "Mom, will I still be four when we get there?"

Our culture is all about instant gratification. I want it and I want it NOW! We eat fast food, we drive fast cars, and we get upset if the computer takes more than 30 seconds to reboot. We want to do everything quicker these days. There's even a church in Pensacola, Florida, that advertises itself as "fast-church." They offer a 22-minute worship service. They have one hymn, one prayer, one scripture reading—but they still make time to take an offering. And then the pastor preaches an eight-minute sermon.

A hundred and fifty years ago if you missed the stagecoach you'd say, "No problem. There will be another stagecoach next week." A hundred years ago if you missed the train you'd say, "No problem, there will be another train tomorrow." Fifty years ago if you missed your flight, you'd think, "No problem, there will be another flight in a few hours." Today if we miss our flight, we're angry if we can't get rebooked in a matter of minutes.

We live in a microwave culture—but you'll never eat a gourmet meal from a microwave. And because of our sinful nature and fast-paced society, we face an increased challenge of living patiently. It's not easy. As I prepared to write this chapter I took a survey of 60 people to ask them to identify situations that try their patience. The top responses fell into three categories that I call "impatience triggers":

Irritating People

People can be irritating, and sometimes those closest to us are the most irritating. We are often more patient with strangers than we are with our own family members. There was once a man in a grocery store pushing a shopping cart with a little boy inside the cart screaming his head off. The man kept his cool and was overheard saying, "Easy, Albert. Take it easy, Albert. Calm down, Albert." A nearby shopper said, "Sir, I want to commend you on how calm and patient you are with little Albert." He said, "Oh, no ma'am. His name is Joe. I'm Albert!"

Waiting In Line

Several people identified the frustration of standing in a long line at a discount store with only a couple of checkers open. Others complained about the long wait in a doctor's office. You wait in the waiting room, and then they take you to a little room to wait alone!

When you get in an "express only" line at the store, do you find yourself counting the items in the cart in front of you to calculate how long it will take? You may be an impatient person.

Two years ago in Saukville, Wisconsin, a woman got in the express check-out lane at the local Piggly Wiggly with more than 10 items. A man behind her accused her of being in the wrong line and continued to verbally harass her until she called the police. They ended up giving the man a ticket right there in the store! I've heard of road rage, but now we have express lane rage!

Traffic

This was the top impatience trigger by far. Do you find yourself irritated when you are behind a car driving 15 miles below the speed limit? When you are in line at a traffic light and it turns green, how long do you wait before you honk your horn at the slow car in front of you? Many people indicated that they often lose their patience in the church parking lot!

There are a lot of crazy drivers out there. A man was driving home from work and his wife called him. She said, "Be careful honey, I heard on the radio that there was an idiot driving in the wrong direction on your road." He said frantically, "There's not just one, there are thousands of them!"

People are impatient drivers. If you don't believe it, try conducting the following experiment. The next time you're the first in line at a red light, wait for three seconds after the light turns green: one Mississippi, two Mississippi, three Mississippi—and see what the car behind you does. But don't try this if I'm the one behind you!

Like all the flavors of the fruit of the Spirit, patience is driven by love. In 1 Corinthians 13 we discover that "Love is patient and kind." When we practice patience, we're showing love to others.

MEMORIZE THIS

"I urge you to live a life worthy of the calling you have received. Be completely humble and gentle; be patient, bearing with one another in love." (Ephesians 4:1–2)

We've learned what patience is and why it's so hard. Now, let's learn HOW we can have patience.

TRUTH #3: PATIENCE IS CALM ENDURANCE UNDER PRESSURE, KNOWING THAT GOD IS IN CONTROL

Sometimes we try to avoid pressure, but pressure can be good. Diamonds are just coal subjected to great pressure over time. The only way we can endure pressure is to have the calm assurance that whatever happens, God is in control.

I recall a story about a man named Bob who went to see his pastor and asked him to pray that he would have more patience. The pastor began to pray, "Father, I pray that you'll fill Bob's life with trouble. Give him trouble in the morning, trouble in the day, and trouble all through the night." Bob, thinking his pastor misunderstood the request, interrupted and said, "I didn't ask you to pray for me to have *trouble*. Pray for me to have *patience*." The pastor smiled and responded, "Son, there's no shortcut for patience. Only trouble and tribulation produce it."

James, the half-brother of Jesus, wrote these powerful words: "Consider it pure joy, my brothers, whenever you face trials of many kinds, because you know that the testing of your faith develops perseverance." (James 1:2–3) The King James Versions says, "The testing of your faith produces patience."

Patience and perseverance are twin virtues. Here's how you can distinguish between them. Patience, as we've pointed out, relates to dealing with difficult people. Perseverance relates to dealing with difficult situations. The word *perseverance* literally means to stay on course. It was used to describe sailors who would "stay under" the North Star when navigating a ship at night. We face the temptation to change course whenever the waves of life are fierce, and the winds of trouble are high. But perseverance keeps us on course, even during a raging storm.

So let's get practical. How can you develop more patience and perseverance? Here are three things you can intentionally do that will improve your PQ (Patience Quotient).

1. **Identify your impatience triggers.** If you know traffic issues are one of your stress points, admit it and work to relieve the stress. Try listening to praise music. Tell yourself to take a deep breath and remember that life isn't about the destination; it's about the journey. Discipline yourself to leave earlier so you

won't have to be in such a hurry. My dad taught me that on time meant 15 minutes early. When you expose your impatience triggers, then you can begin to confront them and deal with them. If you don't know what your impatience triggers are, just ask your spouse or your best friend.

2. **Don't sweat the small stuff.** Some people say, "All stuff is small stuff." And yet there are some big issues that matter, like what you're doing in relation to your Creator. That's big stuff. But most everything else is small stuff. When you find yourself losing patience ask yourself, "One year from now, will _____ matter?" Fill in the blank with whatever problem you are facing. Then ask, "Ten years from now, will this matter?" If that doesn't produce clarity, then ask, "A thousand years from now, will this matter?" Most of the things we lose our patience over don't matter, but the people who are the targets of our impatience DO matter.

3. **Slow down and trust God.** In a fast-paced world, we seldom take time to slow down and enjoy the presence of God. Don't try to drag God along with you at your hectic pace. God isn't in a hurry, even if we are. The psalmist described the chaos of life and how God is our refuge when he wrote in Psalm 46, "God is our refuge and strength, an ever-present help in trouble. Therefore we will not fear, though the earth give way and the mountains fall into the heart of the sea." But then God interrupts and says, "Be still, and know that I am God." (Psalm 46:1–2, 10) When was the last time you got still and sought the presence of God? No phone, no television, no computer—just you and your Creator?

Here are two final observations about patience. First, patience isn't hard; it's impossible. The sooner you admit that, the sooner you will surrender your personality to Jesus, who lives in you to express His perfect patience through you. Let Him work on the inside so that you can express more outward patience with others. That's the key to living a fruitful life. I can't love the unlovely—but Jesus can. I can't have joy when there's heartache—but Jesus can. I can't have peace in the middle of a storm—but Jesus can. And I can't be patient when I'm surrounded by a world that breeds impatience—but Jesus can. Will you let Him fill you with His patience?

Second, understand that God is being patient with you right now, especially if you've heard the Gospel and you haven't yet trusted Christ. The Bible says, "The Lord is not slow in keeping his promise, as some understand slowness. He is patient with you, not wanting anyone to perish, but everyone to come to repentance." (2 Peter 3:9) If you haven't placed your faith in Jesus yet, God is waiting patiently. That's why Jesus hasn't returned. That's why you're still alive. God is incredibly patient.

After the Civil War, the main form of entertainment in America was public speaking. People filled large halls to listen to great orators speak for two or three hours without a microphone. (Sounds like fun, huh? Remember, this was before the onset of radio or television.)

One of the most popular speakers was an atheist named Robert Ingersoll. He loved to blaspheme God and poke fun at Christians and the Bible. His favorite speech was, "Why I am an Agnostic." Once while speaking in Boston he ended his speech with a challenge to prove the existence of God. He said, "If there is a God, I challenge Him to PROVE His existence. If God exists, I invite Him to strike me dead in the next minute." Then he slowly counted down 60 seconds.

There were reports of women fainting and grown men running for the exits for fear that a bolt of lightning would strike down this blasphemer. But at the end of 60 seconds Ingersoll was still standing. He concluded, "So you see, ladies and gentlemen, there is no proof that God exists."

One day a reporter asked Pastor A.J. Gordon what he thought about Robert Ingersoll's challenge to God. Dr. Gordon chuckled and said, "Does Mr. Ingersoll believe he can exhaust God's marvelous patience in just 60 seconds?"

If you haven't trusted Christ yet, God is still patient with you. There is no end to His patience, but there will be an end to your life and to your opportunity to accept His free offer of eternal life. Will you trust Him today?

TAKEAWAY TRUTH
Put What You're Learning Into Practice

How patient are you? Take the following quiz and rate yourself between one and ten. A score of 10 means you have lots of patience. A score of 1 or 0 means you have very little patience.

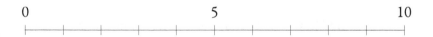

1. **How well do you handle interruptions?** Let's say you're finishing a project at work and someone comes into your office and just wants to chat. When they leave, you're behind schedule. Or you're rushing to get ready to leave home because you're

already late, and the doorbell rings and someone wants to sell you something. What do you typically do?

2. **How do you handle inconveniences?** How do you react when someone sits in "your seat" at church? Or you're driving somewhere and there's a detour or a delay? Will you back up and go a different way, even though it's longer but at least you're moving? How about when you call a service number and there are about 50 automated choices and all you want to do is talk to a person?

3. **How do you handle irritations?** How do you handle irritations like lost keys or computers that decide to stop working? How about the little things that people do that just bug you? My friend Vance Havner said he wouldn't mind being swallowed by a whale, but he hated to be nibbled to death by minnows. What is your response when this happens?

4. **How do you handle inactivity?** Are you a person who can't stand doing nothing? You hate to wait? What do you do when you have absolutely nothing to do?

Total your score here: _____
What is your PQ (Patience Quotient)?

If you scored less than 20, you probably need some more patience in your life. What area do you most need to work on?

If you scored around 30, you're a pretty patient person. Where can you improve?

If you scored 40, then you may be patient, but you may have an honesty problem.

CHAPTER 6

Kiss 'Em With Kindness

Chances are that you've heard the expression, "Kill 'em with kindness." The source that of that phrase comes from Shakespeare's play, *The Taming of the Shrew*. In one scene the scheming Petruchio says of his wife, Kate: "This is a way to kill a wife with kindness; And thus I'll curb her mad and headstrong humour."

I don't really like the phrase, because whether you use anger or kindness, the goal is still to kill someone. Instead I've changed it to "Kiss 'em with kindness."

A man stopped at a highway diner for breakfast. A grumpy waitress came out and said, "What do you want?" He said, "Well, I'd like two eggs, and a few kind words." She didn't say anything before she just turned and left. In a few minutes she returned and slammed down a plate with two greasy eggs. He frowned and asked her, "What about my kind words?" She said, "Don't eat them eggs."

In August 1998 when George H. W. Bush accepted the Republican nomination for president, he said, "I want a kinder, gentler nation." Five months later he was inaugurated as our forty-first President. Do you recall what his first official act was as Chief Executive? He led us in prayer. May God give us more leaders who will lead our nation in prayer.

If it's true of our nation, it's also true of our churches and our homes. We need a kinder, gentler culture.

Sometimes good, religious people can be as mean as a snake. I've had more than one server in a restaurant tell me that the rudest folks are the church people who eat out for Sunday lunch—and they're also the worst tippers! I agree with the little girl who had spent all day with some of these "good, religious people" at church. During her bedtime prayer she prayed, "Dear God, please make all the bad people good. And make all the good people kind."

My favorite definition of kindness is that it is "love with its work clothes on." Patience and kindness appear together in Galatians 5, and there's a reason for that. Patience is passive. It's the ability to NOT blow your stack with difficult people and situations. But kindness is active. Kindness is the act of doing something that demonstrates love, especially to difficult people.

In this chapter I want to lay out a simple sequence for kindness: Know it. See it. Do it. We will examine three cycles of what the Bible says about kindness (Know it). Then I will illustrate this aspect of kindness from three episodes in the life of Jesus (See it). Finally, I'll explore practical ways of how we can demonstrate kindness (Do it).

KNOW IT: *"Be kind and compassionate to one another,*

forgiving each other, just as in Christ God forgave you." (Ephesians 4:32)

The word kindness is *chrestos*, or "grace in action." The Bible teaches that God is full of loving-kindness. He has shown His kindness to us by sending Jesus to die for us. Romans 5:8 says, "God demonstrates his own love for us in this: While we were still sinners, Christ died for us."

On rare occasions, usually when I'm traveling on a plane and the person next to me find out I'm a pastor, someone will say to me, "Oh, I don't believe in God." I've often responded by saying, "Well tell me about this God that you don't believe in." They usually talk about a vindictive, angry God who has failed to heal a family member or who didn't prevent some tragedy. After they finish, I say, "Well, I don't believe in a God like that either." I believe in a God who is kind, loving, and merciful. He will punish sin, and His justice will be satisfied in the future, but now He is opening His arms to anyone who will accept His kindness.

Once a good friend emailed me a funny story about a first-grade boy named Timmy who walked to school with some of his friends every morning. His mother was nervous about Timmy's safety, but she didn't want to embarrass him by walking with him. So she asked her neighbor, Mrs. Goodnest, to walk along behind her son to school as she walked her dog, Marcy.

After several days one of the boys asked Timmy about the woman who seemed to follow them every morning. He said, "Oh, that's my neighbor, Mrs. Goodnest. Her first name is Shirley and that's her dog, Marcy." His friend smirked and said, "Does it bother you that she follows us around?"

Timmy said, "Not really. It's in the Bible. Every night my mom reads the 23rd psalm to me and it says, 'Shirley Goodnest and Marcy shall follow me all the days of my life!'"

God's goodness, mercy, and kindness ARE with us all the days of our lives. And because He has demonstrated kindness to us when we didn't deserve it, we should show kindness to others.

SEE IT: Jesus showed kindness to a desperate woman

In Luke 8 we read the story of the time Jesus was in a hurry to get to the home of Jairus whose daughter was on the verge of death. Jesus was making His way through a mob when suddenly a desperate woman slipped through the crowd and grabbed the hem of His garment. Jesus stopped and said, "Who touched me?" I imagine Peter rolled his eyes as he said, "Lord, we're in a mob...everybody is touching you!" Jesus explained that He felt power go out of Him when someone touched Him.

This woman had suffered with a blood disorder for 12 years. She was a social and religious outcast because of this problem, and her society considered her an "untouchable." And yet, Jesus stopped and gave her His time, His attention, and His healing. He knew who had touched Him, but He wanted her to confess Him before the crowd. When she timidly admitted what had happened, Jesus said, "Woman, your faith has healed you."

Every day we encounter desperate people who reach out to interrupt us while we're on our way somewhere else. Many of them are what our society calls "untouchables." We tend to ignore them, but Jesus didn't. He showed them kindness, and when Jesus lives in us, we'll show kindness to desperate people also.

DO IT: Treat others the way God treats you

We don't deserve God's kindness and we can't really repay Him. The most valuable kindness is when we are kind to strangers or to those who mistreat us.

Years ago, there was a viral video where three middle-school boys tormented Karen Klein, a 68-year-old school bus monitor. They harassed her about her weight and even taunted her about her son having committed suicide "because of her." One of the boys posted the video on YouTube thinking other people would laugh at them making fun of her. His plan backfired. The boys were seen as insulting idiots, and Karen became a hero for anyone who suffers from bullying.

Karen showed amazing patience with those young men and said later, "I wanted to punch [them] is what I wanted to do, so that's why I stayed laid back and just tried to ignore it, because I really wanted to hurt them, you know, and you can't do that. Nope."

That's patience. But since the video was posted, there has been an outpouring of kindness toward Karen, including over $700,000 in online donations from 84 countries and over 32,000 people so she could retire and have a nice life away from her bus route. She didn't press charges, and she has said she forgives the boys.

Let's look at another example of how we can Know It, See It, and Do It when it comes to kindness.

KNOW IT: *"If your enemy is hungry, give him food to eat; if he is thirsty, give him water to drink. In doing this, you will heap burning coals on his head, and the Lord will reward you."* (Proverbs 25:21–22)

Paul quotes this verse in Romans 12:20 when he writes about repaying good for evil. What does it mean to "heap burning coals on his head"? In this case, this simply means when you show kindness to those who treat you like dirt, they end up burning with shame. Someone has said it this way, "Love your enemies. It will drive them crazy." But don't miss the second result of showing kindness to your enemy—God will reward you.

If you are kind to those who are kind to you, that's not true kindness; that's just courtesy. It's kindness when you show mercy to strangers, or to those who have mistreated you, or to those who have no chance of repaying your kindness. That is the true fruit of kindness that results when Jesus is working on the inside, changing your personality.

SEE IT: Jesus showed kindness to an enemy

The night before Jesus was crucified, He was praying in the Garden of Gethsemane. A mob arrived to arrest Jesus, led by Judas. Imagine—he walked up to Jesus and kissed Him in the ultimate act of betrayal. With that signal, the soldiers started grabbing at Jesus. Simon Peter pulled out a sword to defend his master. He boldly slashed at the head of one of the members of the mob, but since Peter was a fisherman, not a swordsman, he missed his head and cut off the man's ear. All four gospel accounts relate this incident, but John identifies the man as being Malchus, a servant of the high priest.

Put yourself in Malchus' sandals for a moment. You've been told this Jesus is a traitor and an imposter. And in the heat of the battle to arrest Him, one of His men cuts off your ear. Suddenly, you think your life is over because people with physical deformities couldn't enter the Temple—and certainly a deformed man could not work for the Jewish high priest. What would your family think? Would your children be afraid of you? But in that moment of pain and fear, the man you were there to arrest does the impossible. He looks into your eyes with kindness, picks up your ear, and places it back on the side of your head. Suddenly the sounds of men talking and fighting rush into your ear canal once more and you can hear. You reach up and touch your ear—it's completely restored. If ever Jesus demonstrated the principle of loving your enemies, it was this night.

DO IT: Bless mean people; don't burn them!

If we're not careful, our motive for showing kindness to mean people can be to wound them. If you perform an act of kindness to someone who has mistreated you, you'll be tempted to think, "Oh yeah. I got them back. I can't wait to see 'em burn with shame. Burn baby, burn! Look at that smoke rising up from their heads. I really showed them." That's not kindness, that's meanness.

We should show kindness to our enemies and to strangers in order to bless them, not to shame them. Roberto De Vicenzo is a Hall of Fame golfer from Argentina who has won over 200 tournaments worldwide. He is most famous for signing an incorrect scorecard in the 1968 Masters. Instead of going into a playoff with Bob Goalby, his mistake put him in second place and Goalby won a green jacket... all because of a scorecard error.

But there's another lesser-known story about De Vicenzo from 1957 when he won first place in a tournament. After being presented the winning check of $5,000 (which was a lot of money back then), he walked back to his car and a woman approached him in the parking lot. She told him that her child was near death in the hospital and she couldn't afford to pay for the treatment. Roberto took pity on her and endorsed his winning check over to her on the spot.

The next week he was approached by a PGA official who had been told by the attendants in the parking lot of Roberto's encounter with the woman. The official said, "I have news for you. She's a phony and has no sick baby. She fleeced you, my friend."

Roberto was silent a moment and then asked, "You mean there is no baby who is dying?" The official shook his head in anger and said, "That's right, I'm sorry to say." Roberto broke out into a big smile and said, "That's the best news I've heard all week!"

Most of us are so cynical and skeptical. We think everyone who is needy is going to take advantage of us. And they might. But we're not the ones who are keeping score; God is. Some of you reading this may still think, "But that woman tricked him. She didn't DESERVE his kindness." I could remind you that none of us deserves the kindness and forgiveness of God. Jesus said that we are to show kindness even to those who are our enemies. In Matthew 5 He explained, "If all you do is love the lovable, do you expect a bonus? Anybody can do that. If you simply say hello to those who greet you, do you expect a medal? Any run-of-the-mill sinner does that." (Matthew 5:46–47 *The Message*)

MEMORIZE THIS

Jesus said, "But love your enemies, do good, and lend, hoping for nothing in return; and your reward will be great, and you will be sons of the Most High. For He is kind to the unthankful and evil." (Luke 6:35–36 NKJV)

Jesus explained the logic very well. If you only show love to those who love you, there's nothing special about that. Can you think of someone right now who has been mean to you? They have mistreated you in the past? Your easiest response—and one that you'll find plenty of other people are doing—is to have nothing to do with them. But I suggest that you do something unusual. Something powerful. Something that can change your life and theirs forever. Be kind to them, not to make them burn with shame, but to bless them. If you do, God will reward your kindness—He says so in His Word.

Booker T. Washington, the first president of Tuskegee Institute, faced a great deal of hatred and abuse as he worked to educate African Americans during the time of Jim Crow Laws in the South. Through it all, he demonstrated the kindness of Christ to his enemies. He once wrote: "I will not allow any man to make me lower myself by hating him. The only way I can destroy my enemy is to make him my friend."

That is another great example of the pattern of kindness described in the Bible. Let me share with you one more.

KNOW IT: *Jesus said, "Anyone who gives you a cup of water in my name because you belong to Christ will certainly not lose his reward."* (Mark 9:41)

Even a small act of kindness has value when you do it in Jesus' name. There's a secular movement in America called Random Acts of Kindness. There's even a Random Acts of Kindness week. For Christians, every week should be Intentional Acts of Kindness in Jesus' Name week. If we perform acts of kindness in the name of a social movement, or worse yet in our name, we receive the glory. But when we perform acts of kindness in Jesus' name, He gets the glory and we receive His reward.

There was a woman in Louisville, Kentucky, who was standing at a bus stop. She had just cashed her tax refund check, so she was carrying more money than usual. The woman glanced around nervously and noticed a shabbily dressed man standing nearby. As she watched, another man walked up to him, handed him some money, and whispered something in his ear. She was so touched by the act of kindness that she decided to do the same. In a burst of generosity, she reached into her purse, took out $10, handed it to the man, and whispered to him, "Never despair, never despair."

The next day when she came to the bus stop, the same shabbily dressed man was there again. But this time he walked up to her and handed her a $100 bill. Dumbfounded, she asked, "What's this?" He said, "You won, lady. Never Despair paid 10 to 1 at Churchill Downs yesterday!"

Kindness does pay off, but not usually in this way. We are kind because we want to give honor and glory to Jesus without expecting anything in return.

SEE IT: Jesus showed kindness to an outcast

In Luke 19 Jesus had an encounter with a vertically-challenged man named Zacchaeus. The people in Jericho hated Zach because he was a tax collector and had gotten rich by cheating them out of their money. But Zach had an itch in his heart that money couldn't scratch. When Jesus arrived in Jericho, Zach was so desperate to see Him that he hoisted himself up on a tree branch to see over the crowd. Adults usually don't climb trees unless they're being chased by a dog, or, as in this case, they are desperate for help. His desperation was palpable.

Jesus could have pointed up in the tree and embarrassed Zach for his misdeeds. He could have said, "Zacchaeus, you're a dirty rotten sinner. Repent, or you're going to hell!" But He didn't do that because the Bible says that Jesus didn't come into the world to condemn sinners, but that through Him sinners could be saved. He said, "Zach, come down from the tree, we're having supper at your house." Over the meal, God changed Zach's heart. Without Jesus having to lecture him on being a good businessman, Zach promised to pay back what he had stolen, plus interest. Jesus then declared, "Today, salvation has come to this house." Do you see what kindness can do in the life of another person?

DO IT: Kindness in Jesus' name can point people to salvation

Jesus said the world would know we are His followers by our love. The world is not going to see Jesus until they first see our kindness. Remember, the world needs a kinder and gentler society today. The world isn't interested in WHAT we believe. They just want to know if it has changed our lives. To put it another way, "People don't care what you know until they know that you care."

The kindest thing you can do for a person is to introduce him or her to Jesus. And sometimes the easiest way to do it is by performing some act of kindness for them in Jesus' name. Kindness is an evangelistic tool. You may not know the four spiritual laws to share with someone the plan of salvation, but you can show kindness in Jesus' name.

In his book *The Conspiracy of Kindness* Steve Sjogren writes: "For most Christians, doing evangelism is a lot like going to the dentist; no one really enjoys doing it, but it must be done once in a while. But anyone can do simple acts of kindness...People don't necessarily remember what they are TOLD of God's love, but they never forget what they have EXPERIENCED of God's love."

In 1956 a poorly dressed young man walked onto the lot of a Cadillac dealer in Tennessee. He was wearing dirty overalls and muddy boots. His hair was sticking out from under an old hunting cap and looked as if it had not been brushed in many days. He walked around the lot for a few minutes, and the salesmen inside watched from the window and made fun of the country hick looking at their expensive Cadillacs. Finally, the manager put a stop to the joking and forced the newest salesman to go outside and ask the bum to leave the car lot.

Instead of kicking him out, the salesman greeted the stranger with kindness and patiently answered all his questions about the cars. After a few minutes the man asked if the dealership would take cash or check. The salesman smiled and said, "Sir, either is fine."

Then the man pointed to one of the cars and said, "Fine. I'll pay cash for this model in every color you make." The "bum" was Elvis Presley and he bought six Cadillacs that day. The salesman's kindness paid off because kindness always pays great dividends.

Stephen Grellet was an unknown missionary who died in 1855. He would have died in obscurity except for one paragraph he wrote that has been quoted thousands of times. He wrote, "I shall pass through this world but once. Any good, therefore, that I can do, or any kindness that I can show to any human being, let me do it now. Let me not defer nor neglect, for I shall not pass this way again." Everyone you meet today is facing some kind of battle. You may never see that person again—will you take the chance to be kind to him or her?

Have you figured out how Jesus works inside of you to produce outward change? Fruit is the outward manifestation of the inner nature. When you see a banana hanging on a tree, you know it's a banana tree. When you see these nine traits in someone's personality, you know that they are a Jesus person. There's one fruit of the Spirit, and it has nine flavors. You can't pick and choose, and say, "I'll take joy, but I'll pass on patience." It's a packaged deal. In this next chapter, we will add to the list of personality traits and include the fruit of goodness.

TAKEAWAY TRUTH
Put What You Are Learning Into Practice

Your goal this week is to let Jesus show His kindness to others through you. Pray:

"Lord, use my eyes to be Your eyes of compassion."

"Lord, use my mouth to speak Your words of kindness."

"Lord, use my hands and my heart to show Your kindness to those who need it most but can't pay me back."

At the end of the week, spend some time reflecting on how these prayers refocused your attention on what is most important.

CHAPTER 7

For Goodness Sake!

We tend to lump people into categories of good and bad. Think of the following people and quickly determine whether you think they are good or bad: Adolph Hitler? Ronald Reagan? Osama bin Laden? Mother Teresa? Joseph Stalin? Coach Tom Landry? Bonnie and Clyde? Billy Graham? President Donald Trump? Goodness isn't always as clear-cut as we may think.

What makes something or someone good? The first time we see the word in the Bible is in the first chapter of Genesis. As God was creating the universe, there were six times He created a portion of all that exists and He saw that it was good.

But when God looked at Adam alone in the Garden of Eden He said, "It is NOT good for man to be alone." I imagine that the conversation between Adam and God went something like this. God said, "Adam, have I got a deal for you! I'm going to give you a wife and she is going to be perfect. She will always look great, and every night she'll massage your neck and cook delicious meals. She will never nag or complain. In other words, she's going to be perfect."

Adam said, "That sounds good, but what is it going to cost me?"

God said, "It's going to cost you an arm and a leg."

Adam thought for a minute and said, "What can I get for just a rib?"

Of course, it didn't happen that way. God put Adam to sleep and took his spare rib and made it into a prime rib called Eve. When Adam saw her for the first time he cried, "Whoa! Man!" So she was called *woman*. And the Bible says God saw that it was VERY good. But what does it mean to be good? The Bible describes it as our next flavor of the fruit of the Spirit, so let's look more closely at what goodness really means.

"I WANT TO BE GOOD!"

It would be easy to pass over this fruit because the word is rather weak in our vocabulary. We throw the word "good" around a lot. Here are some of the ways we use it: Good morning; have a good day; good night; good job; good game; good luck; good luck with that; good move; good hair day; good to know; good to go; good looking; looking good; the good life; good clean fun; good idea; good to see you; it's all good; feeling good; looks good to me; that's not good; so far so good; it's too good to be true; a good time was had by all; for good measure; good riddance; it does my heart good; your guess is as good as mine; it's for your own good. And if you got all that: good for you!

From the start, our parents tell us to be good little boys and girls.

When I was a teenager I went through a rebellious time, and I can recall my mother saying whenever I left home to hang out with my buddies, "Now be good and have fun." At that time, I thought that being good and having fun were two totally opposite things!

Wanting to be good is a worthy goal. Author George Orwell wrote: "On the whole, human beings want to be good, but not too good, and not quite all of the time." That quote reminds me of the mischievous little boy who prayed for God to make him just good enough that he didn't get a spanking.

Let's start with a proper definition of goodness. **I believe goodness is doing the right thing for the right reason.** You can do the right thing, but if you're not doing it for the right reason, that's not goodness. For instance, Jesus warned against the Pharisees who gave their offering in front of others just so they could be seen being generous. They would blow a horn and make a big show out of giving money to a beggar. The reason they did it was so that their peers would see how "good" they were. That's not goodness; it's pure selfishness. Seeing this, Jesus said to His disciples not to draw attention to themselves when they performed good deeds.

If you give your money to help someone on the street, make sure you're doing so out of a sincere sense of compassion, not to enhance your reputation. Going to church is a really good thing to do, but make sure you're doing it for the right reason. Are you there to meet and worship God? Or are you there because you think it will increase your business contacts or that people will see you and think how holy you are? Goodness is doing the right thing for the right reason.

The Bible is the Good Book because it has a lot to say about what is good. The Greek word for *good* is *agathos* and it appears over 250 times in the New Testament. The Hebrew word for good is *tov* and it appears over 350 times in the Old Testament. Whenever I visit Israel, we teach the groups I'm leading to use the Hebrew word because the way you say "good morning" in Hebrew is "boker tov" which is literally "morning good." Some Texans who travel with us have a hard time remembering that, so I tell them instead of saying, "boker tov" just say, "broken toe" because it sounds kind of like it!

God gives us three guidelines for goodness in His Good Book. The prophet Micah wrote, "He has showed you, O man, what is good. And what does the Lord require of you? To act justly and to love mercy and to walk humbly with your God." (Micah 6:8)

To act justly means you treat all people with fairness, honesty, and integrity. Some say "honesty is the best policy," but for a follower of Jesus, honesty is the only policy. Loving mercy means showing mercy to those who most need your mercy. The word mercy in Hebrew means unexpected kindness.

In the last chapter I mentioned that true kindness isn't being kind to someone who can repay your kindness—that's just swapping. True kindness is shown to those who have no way of repaying your kindness. Do you love mercy? Justice and mercy both direct us how to live in relationship with each other.

But God saved the best for last in this verse. The "best good" you can do is walk humbly with God. You can't approach God with arrogance or by making demands that He treat you a certain way. When subjects in biblical time approached a king, they had to bow down as they neared the throne, looking only at the floor. If the king directed them to stand and speak, they could look into his eyes. That's the way we approach the King of Kings, humbly with our heads bowed. But there's a great promise that says, "Humble yourselves, therefore, under God's mighty hand, that he may lift you up in due time." (1 Peter 5:6). In Hebrews we're also told that because of the blood of Jesus, we may boldly approach the throne of grace.

So based on God's three guidelines for goodness, how good are you? If you think you're pretty good, then pay close attention to this next truth.

"BUT I CAN'T BE GOOD!"

We think we're good because we compare ourselves to others. We look at our neighbors, our co-workers, and our friends to measure ourselves. If we're a little better than them, we feel we're pretty good people. The problem is that we're using the wrong standard when we do this. God's standard is perfect goodness and complete holiness. If you use the wrong standard, then all comparison is useless.

I heard a funny story about two brothers named Bob and Old Tom. They were the meanest, most dishonest, conniving men in the county—gamblers, moonshiners, and robbers who never darkened the door of the local church. Old Tom died one day, and Bob asked the Baptist preacher to preach his funeral. The pastor agreed because conducting funerals was part of his job. But then Bob said, "Preacher, during the funeral I want you to say, 'Old Tom was a saint.'" The preacher balked at that request and said, "Bob, I can't do it. Everybody in town knows what a mean scoundrel your brother was." Still, Bob pleaded with the preacher and even promised to donate $10,000 to the building program if he would just say it. With that, the preacher agreed.

The church was packed for the funeral because everyone wanted to see what the preacher would say about notorious Old Tom. As the preacher opened his Bible he drew a deep breath and said, "Folks, you know that Old Tom was a mean-spirited, wicked man who never had time for God. You know that Tom was a drunkard and a liar. And he was as mean as a snake." The crowd sat in stunned silence, and Bob started to get up from his seat to collar the preacher. Then the preacher pointed to Bob and said, "But compared to his brother Bob, Old Tom was a saint!"

Some people read Jesus' Sermon on the Mount and try to live by those principles, and if they do, they think they're pretty good. After Jesus gave all the beatitudes, He talked about murder, divorce, adultery, and revenge, and loving your enemies. Some people use those as a checklist to check off their obedience in those areas. If they can check all the boxes, they think, "I'm pretty good." But don't miss what Jesus said next. He said, "Be perfect, therefore, as your heavenly father is perfect." (Matthew 5:48)

Some people can be good most of the time, and most people can be good some of the time. But no person can be perfectly good all of the time. So before you start talking about how good you are, look at these words from the Bible, "There is no one who does good, not even one...I know that nothing good lives in me, that is, in my sinful nature. For I have the desire to do what is good, but I cannot carry it out." (Romans 3:12; 7:18)

Can you relate to that? I think all of us desire to be good and to do good; but we have this anchor called a sinful nature that keeps dragging us back down. You'll never find true forgiveness and goodness until you ADMIT you don't have the capacity to be good. The Bible says this about my heart and yours, "The heart is deceitful above all things, and desperately wicked; who can know it?" (Jeremiah 17:9 NKJV) The Bible says, "The wicked are estranged from the womb; they go astray as soon as they are born, speaking lies." (Psalm 58:3 NKJV)

My experiences as a parent and a grandparent confirm that children aren't born inherently good—they are born with a full-grown selfish, sinful nature. They don't have to be taught to steal; they have to be taught NOT to steal. They don't have to be taught to lie; they have to be taught NOT to lie.

Many people I've known are in denial about this truth. Years ago I listened to a heartbroken mother cry her eyes out because her son had been arrested for the third time for dealing drugs and he was heading to prison. To this day, I can still her say, "But deep down inside, he is a good boy."

I didn't correct her, but I was thinking, "No. Deep down inside, he's like the rest of us. He's a bad boy." I've heard abused wives excuse their husband's violent behavior by saying something like, "But he's a good man at heart." No ma'am. He's a bad man at heart. All humans are. We want to be good, but we can't be good on our own.

"JESUS IS GOOD FOR ME AND HE'S GOOD IN ME!"

In Mark 10 a rich young ruler came to Jesus and asked, "Good teacher, what must I do to inherit eternal life?" Before Jesus answered his question, He posed one of His own: "Why do you call me good? No one is good—except God alone."

One of the first prayers we teach our children contains two powerful statements about the nature and character of God. We pray, "God is great. God is good. Let us thank Him for our food." Both of those affirmations are bedrock truths about our Heavenly Father. We have a saying in our church: "God is good all the time...and all the time God is good." The Bible affirms this many times. Psalm 34:8 says, "Taste and see that the Lord is good; blessed is the man who takes refuge in him." Psalm 86:5 says, "You are forgiving and good, O Lord, abounding in love to all who call to you." We read in Psalm 106:1, "Give thanks to the Lord, for he is good; his love endures forever."

So if God is good, what does that have to do with you? When you came to Christ, Jesus took up residence in your heart through the person of the Holy Spirit. And He went to work. You now have access to this divine goodness that can transform your personality. Remember, it's not your futile attempts at goodness that change you; it's the goodness of Jesus shining out through you. Let me illustrate this with an important event in the Old Testament.

In Exodus 33:18 Moses was on Mt. Sinai receiving the Ten Commandments from God when he made a strange request. Moses said, "Show me your glory." In other words, Moses wanted to see God face-to-face. However, God explained, "If you looked at my face, you would die on the spot. But here's what I will do. I will let my *goodness* pass in front of you." Did you catch that? Moses asked to see God's glory, and God said His glory is best seen in His goodness. I'm not sure how this transpired, but when the goodness of God passed by Moses, he had to take shelter in a cleft of a rock or it would be too much for him to take. Even a glimpse of the afterglow of God's goodness made the face of Moses radiate from within. You've heard that pregnant mothers sometimes have a "glow" about them. Or you may see a young couple in love whose faces seem to glow with happiness when they spend time together. I imagine that was sort of like Moses' experience—there was something special about him after he encountered God this way. But Moses wasn't aware that his face was shining until he went back down to the people and they pointed it out to him. In fact, Moses had to wear a veil to cover the radiance that came from seeing God's electrifying goodness so that he could talk to the people.

In the New Testament, Paul picks up on this idea and compares us to Moses. He explains that unlike Moses, we can be with God, but we don't have to wear a veil. He writes, "And we, who with unveiled faces all reflect the Lord's glory, are being transformed into his likeness with ever-increasing glory, which comes from the Lord, who is the Spirit." (2 Corinthians 3:18) Just as the radiance of God was shining out from Moses, the powerful goodness of Jesus can shine out through our lives. We don't need to cover it up. Instead, God wants us to let it shine, let it shine, let it shine!

Walking in the Spirit is a daily, continual experience of being transformed into the likeness of Jesus. When I allow His personality to fill my personality, other people will see goodness in me.

At funerals you often hear preachers say, "He was a good man" or, "She was a good woman." What is the key to being recognized as a good man or a good woman? We find the answer in a description of one of the early Christians named Barnabas. The Bible says, "He (Barnabas) was a good man, full of the Holy Spirit." (Acts 11:24) Those aren't two separate descriptions of the same man; they are connected. Barnabas was a good man BECAUSE he was full of the Holy Spirit.

Before Jesus was crucified, He promised the disciples to send them the Holy Spirit to take His place and be close to them. Jesus said, "I have been with you, but He will be in you." Before Pentecost and the arrival of the Holy Spirit, the disciples could only watch Jesus and try to imitate His personality and actions in their own strength. How frustrating that must have been! But after the Holy Spirit came, they were filled with the Spirit of Jesus. No longer did they have to try imitating Jesus with hit and miss success. Now His personality dwelled within them. And we have the same resource today. If you will concentrate on allowing the Holy Spirit of Jesus to fill you every day, then you will be good—not in your own power but in His.

MEMORIZE THIS

"For we are God's workmanship, created in Christ
Jesus to do good works, which God prepared
in advance for us to do." (Ephesians 2:10)

God's plan for your life is that you will do good in this world. The Bible says, "For by grace are ye saved **through** faith...created in Christ Jesus **unto** good works..." Ephesians 2:8–10 KJV. Don't confuse those prepositions. Good works don't save us; we are saved UNTO good works, which means our salvation ushers us into a life of goodness. Good works can never EARN salvation, but they are EVIDENCE of our salvation. If you are a Christian, you will be doing good things. But you can't boast about them because it's not your goodness—it's God's.

In other words, good works are not the root of salvation; they are the fruit of salvation. Jesus said in Matthew 5:16, "Let your light shine before men..." When people look at you and the goodness you exhibit—are they giving you the credit for being such a kind, compassionate, giving, thoughtful person? Are they giving you the glory for who you appear to be? Or are they giving the glory and credit to God who works inside of you to do good things?

One of my television heroes growing up was Sheriff Andy Taylor from Mayberry on *The Andy Griffith Show*. Sheriff Andy Taylor was a good guy and a single dad who attended church on Sunday and even sang in the choir. Somehow he also demonstrated amazing patience with the bungling deputy Barney Fife. I think this was an easy role for Andy Griffith the actor to play because Andy was a committed follower of Jesus. His wife, Cindi, posted this statement after his death: "Andy was a person of incredibly strong Christian faith and was prepared for the day he would be called home to his Lord. I cannot imagine life without Andy, but I take comfort and strength in God's grace and in the knowledge that Andy is at peace and with God."

My very favorite episode was when Barney and Andy had to eat Aunt Bea's homemade pickles, even though they tasted like kerosene. But there was another episode that taught a great lesson about goodness. It was called, "The Cave Rescue." The people of Mayberry were laughing at Barney Fife because early that morning he tried to arrest the bank president who was unlocking the door to his own bank.

In order to make him forget the humiliation, Andy planned a picnic for Barney, Thelma Lou, and Helen. During the picnic, Andy and Helen wandered off to explore Lost Lovers Cave. There was a cave-in and Barney realized Andy and Helen were trapped. So he organized a massive rescue effort. Meanwhile, Andy and Helen found a way out of the cave through another opening and hitchhiked back into town to clean up at Helen's house.

While listening to the radio, they heard a news bulletin about two people trapped in a cave near Mayberry and how Deputy Barney Fife had organized a massive rescue effort to save them. Helen picked up the phone to call the courthouse and tell them to call off the search. But Andy stopped her. He said that if the townspeople knew they were safe, Barney would become even more of a joke to his fellow citizens.

In order to prevent further ridicule directed at Barney, they put their dirty clothes back on and rushed back into the cave through the back entrance. They rubbed dirt on their faces and sat down as if they were exhausted just a few moments before the rescue party discovered them. Barney became the hero because of Andy's sense for doing the right thing for the right reason.

Goodness won't get you into heaven. Only Jesus can! Ask the average person on the street how to go to heaven and the number one answer is still some variance of: "Be good. Do good." The problem is that we just don't have the human capacity for perfect goodness. We need to depend on the goodness and grace of someone better than us—and that Someone is Jesus. Here's what the Bible says in John 3:16 about how you can go to heaven because of Him:

"For God so loved the world [substitute your name for "world"], that He gave His one and only Son; that whoever [put your name here] believes in Him, will not perish, but will have eternal life."

The only good thing you need to do to spend eternity in heaven is to simply BELIEVE that Jesus is the only One who can take you there, and then trust Him to do it. Have you done so already? Good for you!

TAKEAWAY TRUTH

Put What You Are Learning Into Practice

This week do something kind in Jesus' name for someone else, but make sure you don't get the credit for it. Be creative. And pray about what you plan to do. Afterwards, spend some time reflecting:

How did it feel to do something for someone else?

How easy or difficult was it to remain anonymous?

CHAPTER 8

Faithfulness: A Long Obedience In The Same Direction

'm borrowing the title of this chapter on faithfulness from Eugene Peterson. He is best known for his paraphrase of the Bible, *The Message*, but he has written a number of excellent books as well. One of his earliest books is entitled *A Long Obedience in the Same Direction: Discipleship in an Instant Society*. The title itself has fascinated me for years.

But Eugene Peterson didn't invent that phrase; he borrowed it from Friedrich Nietzsche. If you're thinking you recognize that name as a linebacker for the Green Bay Packers, you're mistaken. That was Ray Nitschke. Friedrich Nietzsche was a German philosopher. In one of his books he wrote: "The essential thing in heaven and earth is that there should be a long obedience in the same direction; there results, and has always resulted in the long run, something which has made life worth living."

Of course, Nietzsche is best known for starting the "God is Dead" movement. Nietzsche died in 1900, so you might have seen the quote that says, "God is dead. Nietzsche, 1883. Nietzsche is dead. God, 1900."

Even though Nietzsche was wrong about God being dead, his phrase "A long obedience in the same direction" is a winner. That's a simple definition of the spiritual fruit of faithfulness.

Have you ever thought about how important the word *faithful* is? In order to illustrate it, let me ask you a trivia question. The category is US history. When was the last time we had no legally sworn-in President of the United States?" The correct answer is January of 2008. Here's what happened. Our U.S. Constitution mandates that the Oath of Office for the President should read: "I do solemnly swear that I will FAITHFULLY execute the Office of the President of the United States." At President Barack Obama's inauguration on January 20, 2008, he placed his hand on the same Bible that Lincoln used for his Oath of Office and prepared to repeat the oath after Chief Justice John Roberts. But the Chief Justice made a mistake when administering the oath. He led President Obama to say, "I do solemnly swear that I will execute the Office of the President of the United States FAITHFULLY."

You may be thinking, "That's no big deal." Well, it *was* a big deal. The Justice Department advised that unless the oath is repeated exactly as it appears in the Constitution, it is not binding. So, it wasn't until 32 hours later the next day in a private ceremony inside the White House that President Obama correctly repeated the Oath of Office, and he put the word faithfully in the right place. Some have pointed out that he didn't use a Bible for the do-over. But that's not a Constitutional requirement. Here's a bonus trivia answer—three other presidents didn't swear on the Bible: John Quincy Adams, Teddy Roosevelt, and Lyndon Johnson.

In this chapter, I want to examine faithfulness from two perspectives. First, we'll discover God's faithfulness toward us. Then we'll explore our faithfulness toward God.

WE TRUST THAT GOD IS FAITHFUL TO US

Like all the other flavors of the fruit of the Spirit, faithfulness is not something we have to manufacture ourselves. It is part of the character and nature of our God.

We don't read the book of Lamentations very much because it's depressing. Seriously. It contains the expressions of misery of the weeping prophet, Jeremiah. But amid the darkness of his soul, Jeremiah was able to see the brilliant faithfulness of God shining into his heart.

MEMORIZE THIS

"Because of the Lord's great love we are not consumed, for his compassions never fail. They are new every morning; great is your faithfulness." (Lamentations 3:22–23)

In 1923 Thomas Chisholm blazed the new Chisholm Trail by writing a poem about God's faithfulness. It was later put to music and has become one of the most beloved hymns of all time. Despite the King James language, the words are still beautiful in *Great Is Thy Faithfulness*.

As I was learning this hymn as a child, I would often confuse the "Thy" with "my" and found myself singing, "Great is *my* faithfulness." But that's not what it says! It says, "Great is *thy* faithfulness." There are many times when we may not be faithful to the Lord, but there has never been a moment when He has not been faithful to us.

The Bible says in 2 Timothy 2:13, "When we are faithless, He remains **faithful**." First John 1:9 reminds us, "He is **faithful** and just to forgive us our sins." In 1 Corinthians 10:13, God's Word says, "God is **faithful** and will not allow us to be tempted beyond what we are able, but will with the temptation, give us a way to escape." Psalm 86:5 reminds us that "God is abounding in love and **faithfulness**." And Psalm 100:5 declares, "God's **faithfulness** continues through all generations."

Our God is faithful! But you have to transfer that understanding from your head to your heart. You have to TRUST that He is faithful. Sometimes when trouble and tragedy afflict us we wonder what God is doing. But these are the very times when we have to TRUST that God is faithful to keep His promises to us. As the prophet Jeremiah wrote, "He has a plan for your life—a plan to prosper you, not to hurt you; a plan to give you hope and a future." (Jeremiah 29:11)

WE KNOW THAT GOD REWARDS OUR FAITHFULNESS

God not only admires faithfulness but He also requires our faithfulness. In His message to the church at Smyrna Jesus said, "Be faithful, even to the point of death, and I will give you the crown of life." (Revelation 2:10) We learn two things from that verse. First, faithfulness may cost us everything—even our lives. Second, God will reward us for our faithfulness.

Have you ever visited the Old Faithful geyser in Yellowstone National Park? There are larger and more powerful geysers, yet this one remains the most famous of all because of its predictability. If the previous eruption lasts less than 2.5 minutes, the next one will occur 65 minutes later. If the eruption lasts more than 2.5 minutes, the next eruption will happen 91 minutes later. You can set your watch by it.

Other geysers are unpredictable and cannot be safely approached. But when Old Faithful was named in 1870, soldiers used it for their laundry because they knew when it would erupt. They would safely walk up to it and put their dirty clothes in the geyser and wait. They found out the hard way that linen and cotton clothing would be shot into the air clean, but wool clothing was torn to shreds.

Old Faithful just keeps spewing along day after day, week after week, and year after year. Let me give you another word for faithfulness. It's good old-fashioned "stick-to-it-ivness." That may not be a word, but when you need a word and can't find a word you make up a word. Faithfulness isn't just doing the right thing once; it's doing the right thing over and over again, day after day, week after week, year after year—just like Old Faithful. A good synonym for faithfulness is loyalty. How loyal are you? Like every other variety of fruit, we can't manufacture faithfulness. But when we surrender to Jesus, who lives in us, His faithfulness will be displayed in our lives because He is at work on our personality. Let's consider some practical areas where we can increase our faithfulness quotient.

1. Through Jesus I can be a loyal family member

Husbands and wives, are you faithful to each other? Parents, are you faithful to your children? Children, are you faithful to your parents? The traditional family is under attack today in America. The foundation of a nation is the family, and the devil knows that if he can destroy stable families then our nation will fall apart.

When things are great in your family, loyalty comes easy. But when families go through tough times, that's when we need to show even more loyalty to one another. There's a picturesque verse from Proverbs that speaks about the value of loyalty. "Like a bad tooth or a lame foot is reliance on the unfaithful in times of trouble." (Proverbs 25:19)

If you've ever had a toothache, you know that it makes you miserable. If you have a bad foot, every step you take is agony. That's a description of how miserable families are when family members are unfaithful to each other.

2. Through Jesus I can be a loyal friend

You can't choose your family, but you can choose your friends. And if you go through this life with some real friends, then you are rich indeed. The Bible says, "A friend loves at all times, and a brother is born for adversity." (Proverbs 17:17)

A few years ago a national magazine held a contest to ask readers to give a definition of a friend. One of the submissions that won honorable mention said, "A friend is someone who multiplies your joys and divides your sorrows." Another said, "A friend is someone who understands your silence." But the winning entry said very simply, "A friend is someone who walks in when all the world has walked out."

You may be thinking, "I wish I had a friend like that." If you want a friend, you must first BE a friend. Proverbs 18:24 says, "A man that has friends must show himself friendly." (KJV)

3. Through Jesus I can be a loyal manager of God's money

The Bible talks about "stewardship," but we don't have a frame of reference for that word because we no longer have people in our culture who work as stewards. In the old days of England, a steward was a man who ran the estate of a wealthy landowner. The steward lived in the house and used the land owned by another man. His job was to manage it well. If your last name is Stewart, you probably had ancestors who managed a large estate. The word comes from two old English words, *stig*, meaning house and *weard*, which meant guard. A steward was someone who guarded and managed the house of his boss.

All of us are stewards. We don't own anything; we only manage it for our Boss, God. That house you live in? It's not yours. God owns it and you're managing it for Him. That car, those stocks, and bonds? They aren't yours. God owns them all. What kind of manager are you?

Jesus said, "Whoever can be trusted with very little can also be trusted with much, and whoever is dishonest with very little will also be dishonest with much. So if you have not been trustworthy in handling worldly wealth, who will trust you with true riches?" (Luke 16:10–11)

To put it another way, if you're faithful with a little, God will entrust more for you to manage. You may be thinking, "If I had a million dollars, I'd give God 10% of it." Well if God can't trust you to tithe on the $1,000 you make a week, what makes you think He will trust you with more?

This is a powerful truth because most American Christians reverse the order. They think, "If I'm a good spiritual manager, then God will give me riches." Jesus said exactly the opposite. He said that if you're a good manager of God's money, then He will entrust you with true riches. So if "true riches" isn't referring to money, what is He talking about?

True riches, we learn in God's Word, are spiritual blessings. You may think, "If I was more spiritually mature, I would tithe to the Lord." Nope. Turn it around. If you tithe your income to the Lord, you will become more spiritually mature. If you don't believe it, try it. Go ahead and tithe and see what happens. That's what God says in Malachi 3:10. "Bring all the tithes...and see if I will not throw open the windows of heaven and pour out for you so much BLESSING (true riches) that there will not be room enough to receive it." (NKJV)

4. Through Jesus I can be a loyal church member

We need to show loyalty to our family, to our friends, to God, and we should show loyalty to each other by being a part of the local church. The Bible says, "In Christ we who are many form one body, and each member belongs to all the others." (Romans 12:5–6) I belong to you, and you belong to me. I need you, and you need me. We all need each other, so God provided a structure for this relationship and He called it the Church.

As I travel around the world, I notice there are three big "M's" America exports all over the world: music; movies, and McDonald's. Fortunately there is something unique to America that we haven't yet exported to foreign countries—uncommitted Christians. In a typical American church, like the one I have served for almost 30 years, we will have many more members on our rolls than actually attend. For instance, we have over 15,000 members but two-thirds of our members don't even show up on a given Sunday. Plus, in America, there are people who call themselves Christians and attend a church, but they haven't joined as a committed member. They're like "free-floating" Christians.

In contrast, I have discovered in churches around the world that all the believers are connected to a local congregation. They are loyal to their church. In fact, attendance at these churches is always LARGER than their membership. In Asia, Africa, and Central and South America if a church has 100 members, there will be 120 attending. If they have 1,000 members, there will be 1,200 people attending. And in some of the largest churches, if they have 10,000 members they will have 12,000 in attendance. The largest 25 churches in the world aren't in North America. What's the problem? America Christians show very little FAITHFULNESS and loyalty to their church. If you are reading this and you are a faithful attender, I'm not criticizing you. I'm just diagnosing a spiritual problem that exists in American churches.

Imagine joining an army, but then you show up whenever you feel like it, or not at all. And if you do go into battle, when the going gets tough, you leave the battlefield for a safer location. Would you like to share a foxhole with someone like that? The truth is, we are at war. We're involved in spiritual warfare and too many of the soldiers of the Lord are AWOL: Absent Without Love.

But just attending a church isn't enough. Some who only attend but don't serve are like a spectator rather than a participant. In every American church, about 20 percent of the members are doing 80 percent of the work. To which group do you belong? Will you demonstrate your faithfulness to Jesus by stepping up from the crowd to volunteer to be a part of the committed core?

In America, many Christians have opted to watch church services on television rather than attend in person. Televised broadcasts are a wonderful blessing for people who are physically unable to attend church. But if you have the health to attend in person, you need to get out of your recliner and show up at a local church where the Bible is preached. Television is not a substitute for worship because there is no opportunity to do what the Bible says is the reason WHY we gather on Sundays: fellowship. I like Eugene Peterson's paraphrase of Hebrews 10:25. "Let's see how inventive we can be in encouraging love and helping out, not avoiding worshiping together as some do but spurring each other on, especially as we see the big Day approaching." The big Day is the return of Christ, so there's no time to lose. Will you be a loyal church member?

Faithfulness Has a Price

Being faithful isn't cheap. Sometimes it costs us everything. The events that happened on 9/11 weren't the first Islamic jihad attack on Americans. In 1983 the U.S. Marines were stationed in Beirut,

Lebanon, as a peacekeeping force in the Lebanon Civil War. Early on a Sunday morning, a suicide bomber drove a truck through the barbed wire fence surrounding the Marine Corps barracks and detonated an explosive device equal to 12,000 tons of TNT. The building was leveled, and 241 American marines, sailors, and soldiers were killed.

Since that time, there has been ample proof that Iran directly sponsored the attack. In July of 2012 a U.S. Federal Judge ordered Iran to pay more than $813 million in damages to the families of the Marines who lost their lives. Of course, there's no way to make Iran pay.

There were only a handful of survivors, and one of the Marines pulled from the debris was Lance Corporal Jeff Nashton. Terribly injured and blinded by the explosion, he was airlifted to a military hospital in Germany.

General Paul Kelley, Commandant of the Marine Corps, went to visit Corporal Nashton in the hospital to present him a Purple Heart. When he walked into the hospital room, General Kelley said he had never seen that many tubes coming out of one man. He commented that he looked more like a machine than a man. He introduced himself, but since Corporal Nashton was now blind, the soldier didn't believe he was really talking to a general. He thought some of his buddies were playing a trick on him. So he grabbed the general's collar to feel for stars. He felt one, two, three, four stars, and then he released the man and did his best to salute.

Corporal Nashton was unable to speak because of a breathing tube, but he motioned for a piece of paper and a pen to write. He sightlessly scribbled two words on the paper and showed it to the general. He wrote, "Semper Fi." Every Marine knows that stands for "Semper Fidelis," the Marine Corps motto that means, "Always faithful."

The rough, tough general said he felt tears rolling down his cheeks when he looked at the soldier's wounds and read those two words. According to Marine Corps lore, that was the only time General Kelley cried. He saluted the soldier, reached up, and removed the four stars from his collar and pressed them into Corporal Nashton's hand. Then he said, "Here, son, you deserve these more than I do." Corporal Nashton recovered and he keeps those four stars as a constant reminder of "Semper Fi."

"Semper Fi" means never giving up or never giving in. We can say that about Jesus. He was always faithful, even unto death, for us. As followers of Jesus we should always be faithful to Him. Because the Bible says that one the day when we come face to face with Jesus we will want to hear Him say these amazing words, "Well done, good and faithful servant! You have been faithful with a few things; I will put you in charge of many things. Come and share your master's happiness!" (Matthew 25:21)

TAKEAWAY TRUTH

Put What You Are Learning Into Practice

How are you doing practicing faithfulness? Evaluate yourself in the following areas where 0 represents no faithfulness and 4 means you are consistently faithful.

I am a loyal family member.

0   1   2   3   4

I am a loyal friend.

0   1   2   3   4

I am a loyal manager of God's money.

0   1   2   3   4

I am a loyal church member.

0   1   2   3   4

How did you do? What can you do this week to improve in this area? Tell a friend what you will be doing to practice being more faithful and ask him or her to pray for you.

CHAPTER 9

Gentleness: People Are Fragile—Handle With Care

et's review what you have learned so far—we'll start with the basics. When you see an orange hanging on a tree, you can identify that tree as an orange tree. Fruit is the outward expression of an inner nature. Jesus said the same thing about people. He said, "By their fruit you will recognize them." (Matthew 7:16) When you see all nine personality characteristics in someone, you can safely assume that person is filled with the nature of Jesus. In this chapter we'll explore the fruit of gentleness. It is also translated "meekness" in some Bibles. I use both words interchangeably to describe the same fruit.

To better understand a word, it's helpful to know what the opposite meaning is. The opposite of gentleness is violence. Over the past 20 years we have seen an alarming rise in mass shootings in America. Many of them have taken place in our schools and workplaces. That kind of mass violence is the opposite of kindness, goodness, and gentleness. The world without Christ considers gentle people to be weak people, losers, or doormats. A few years ago, Robert Ringer wrote two best-selling books that even encouraged people to be aggressive in the dog-eat-dog business world. He wrote *Winning Through Intimidation* and then he followed it with *Looking Out for #1*. That's the aggressive attitude of the world without Christ. But what the world needs desperately is more gentleness. People are fragile. They must be handled with care.

AM I STRONG ENOUGH TO BE GENTLE?

If you want to learn about gentleness, you must understand that real gentleness requires supernatural strength. In fact, the only way to be gentle is to be filled with the power of the Holy Spirit. Let me clear up two misunderstandings about gentleness or meekness.

1. Gentleness isn't weakness—It's strength under control

The Greek word for meekness and gentleness is *praus*. It's the word Jesus used in the Beatitudes when He said, "Blessed are the meek, for they will inherit the earth." (Matthew 5:5). The best way to understand the meaning of this word is to know how it was used in the Greek language. It didn't mean "weak;" in fact, it was used to describe a wild, powerful horse that had been trained to be ridden.

In Texas we call it "breaking" a horse. A trainer has to break the stubborn, unbridled nature of the horse in order to get it to a place where it will submit to a bridle and a saddle. When the Greeks referred to a horse that had been trained, they used a verb to say the horse had been "meeked." They used the exact word, *praus*, the same word used for the fruit of the Spirit called gentleness.

Corbin Preifert is a delightful friend of mine who is still sharing his faith although he is approaching his departure to heaven. He is the consummate salesman. A few years ago, he invited me to drive him up to Mt. Pleasant, Texas, to visit the Preifert factory where they make farm equipment that is sold all around the world. It was an interesting trip and I got to meet Corbin's nephew, Bill, who now runs the company. I also got to meet Radar, a Belgian draft horse who for a few years held the Guinness World record for being the tallest horse in the world. They measure horses to their shoulders, and Radar's shoulders tower at 6' 7.5 inches, and he weighs around 2,400 pounds. When he lifts his head, he could bump it on a basketball rim. If you attempted to ride Radar, you would need a six-foot stepladder to climb onto his back.

As I walked up to this massive horse, I was amazed by his gentleness. Even though Radar had the strength to hurt me, or even kill me, fortunately, he had been "meeked." He walked over to me and let me rub his huge nose and pat him on his massive neck. His hoofs were as big around as my head; he could have crushed my feet if he had stepped on me. But he was completely gentle—a gentle giant.

That's a powerful picture of meekness—great strength under control. The great Methodist preacher Ralph Sockman wrote, "Nothing is so strong as gentleness. And nothing is more gentle than real strength. It is a soft touch with a strong hand."

2. Gentleness isn't cowardice—It's the courage to surrender

The Bible is full of paradoxes. Jesus said if you try to gain your life you'll lose it, but if you truly lose your life in surrender to Him, that's when you gain your life. When my daughters were growing up we watched the movie *The Princess Bride* so many times that we had memorized many of the lines. (For all you fans: *Hello, my name is Inigo Montoya. You killed my father. Prepare to die.*)

Our favorite character in the movie was Fezzik, played by André the Giant. Andre stood 7' 5 inches tall and weighed over 500 pounds. He first made his name in professional wrestling and for a time was the highest paid wrestler in history. I'm about to give a spoiler alert, so if you don't want to hear it, skip this paragraph. Okay. Here it is: professional wrestling is fake. It's rigged. The same people who think Elvis is still alive also believe professional wrestling is real.

I say that because although André the Giant seemed like a ferocious monster in the wrestling ring, those who knew him best said it was only an act. Outside the ring he was kindhearted and generous. He once refused tickets to a Broadway show because he knew the people sitting behind him wouldn't be able to see, and he didn't want to spoil it for them. André died of congestive heart failure at 47 while in Paris for his father's funeral. Before he died, he said his favorite role was the gentle, loving giant named Fezzik.

Gentleness is displayed when you have the power to subdue someone, but you choose not to. Through the years I have been involved with the Fellowship of Christian Athletics (FCA). In the 1980s I was blessed to be the camp pastor for the National FCA camp in Black Mountain, North Carolina. Other speakers that week were Coach Tom Landry and NFL star Reggie White, both of whom are in heaven now.

But one of my favorite athletes there that week was a guy with a black belt who had a ministry he called Karate for Christ. I can't remember his name, but he put on an amazing demonstration of breaking boards and concrete blocks, and he even jump-kicked a cap off the head of Reggie White, who was over 6' tall. He told us about one night when he had been putting on a demonstration at an inner-city gym in Philadelphia. As he was walking back to his car in an alley, a young man confronted him with a knife and demanded his wallet. As he stood there sizing up his foe, the martial arts expert mentally reviewed several scenarios of how he could easily disarm the thief, break his arm, or even kill him.

He was thinking, "This guy picked the wrong man to try to rob." But then he realized that this kid was pretty scared. So instead of hurting him, he just assumed a fighting stance and yelled, "Hi-YAH!" And then he turned and ran out the other end of the ally! When he turned around, the punk was gone. He had the strength and the skill to hurt that kid, yet he chose not to. Instead, he ran. That's meekness. Sometimes it takes more courage NOT to fight than to fight. You have to choose your battles carefully in life. Someone once said a bulldog can whip a skunk, but it's just not worth the effort.

There aren't many times in the Bible where Jesus describes His own personality type. But we know that Jesus was gentle because that's the way He described Himself.

MEMORIZE THIS

"Take my yoke upon you and learn from me, for I am gentle and humble in heart, and you will find rest for your souls. For my yoke is easy and my burden is light." (Matthew 11:29-30)

WILL YOU ALLOW JESUS TO TRANSPLANT HIS GENTLENESS INTO YOUR PERSONALITY?

When you allow Jesus to transplant His gentleness in you, there are three ways that it will start to take effect in your life.

Gentleness in action

The Bible teaches that God relates to us with the gentleness of a Good Shepherd who leads us. I love this description of our Shepherd: "He tends his flock like a shepherd: He gathers the lambs in his arms and carries them close to his heart; he gently leads those that have young." (Isaiah 40:11)

Do you treat people with the same gentleness? Jesus put the needs of others before His own. That's a mark of gentleness. Self-centered people aren't gentle because they don't consider others as being more important than themselves. New Testament scholar Martyn Lloyd Jones gives us more insight into meekness:

> "The man who is meek is not sensitive about himself. Is it not one of the greatest curses in life as a result of the fall—this sensitivity about self? We spend the whole of our lives watching ourselves. But when a man becomes meek he has finished with all that; he no longer worries about himself and what other people say. The man who is truly meek never pities himself, he is never sorry for himself. He never talks to himself and says, 'You are having a hard time, how unkind these people are not to understand you.' He never thinks: 'How wonderful I really am, if only other people gave me a chance.' Self-pity! What hours and years we waste in this! But the man who has become meek has finished with all that."

A gentle person is so concerned about the needs of others that they never throw a pity party for themselves. The worst thing about a pity party is that you're the only guest—and there are no presents!

Once when I was preaching, I demonstrated gentleness by asking a young boy to join me on the platform. I asked him to shake my hand and squeeze as hard as he could. I jokingly told him to go ahead and try to hurt me. He did his best, but he wasn't strong enough. Then I turned the tables and said, "Okay, now I'm going to squeeze your hand as hard as I can!" Suddenly a look of fear came into his eyes because he knew I was much stronger than him, and I really could have crushed his hand. Instead I gave his hand a gentle but firm grip and said, "This is what gentleness is. I am keeping my strength under control." He relaxed and boy was he relieved!

As far as I can tell, there was only one time when Jesus got good and mad at His disciples. It's in Mark 10 when some parents wanted to bring their young children to Jesus, but the disciples rebuked them. I imagine they probably scolded the parents and said, "Don't you know who this is? Why, He's the most famous traveling rabbi in Israel. He doesn't have time for *you* and your *kids*. He's too busy with important things." When Jesus saw how His disciples spoke to these well-meaning parents, the Bible says He was indignant. He was good and mad and said, "Let the little children come to me. In fact, unless you adults receive the Kingdom like one of these little children, you'll never enter it." Then the Bible says He took the children in His arms, placed His hands on them, and blessed them. That's one of my favorite pictures of the gentleness of Jesus. In His hands resided the power to heal the sick, raise the dead, and to create entire galaxies. They were the strongest hands any man ever had, yet He was gentle enough to caress little children.

Gentleness isn't weakness; it's strength under control. Gentleness means you don't use your strength to hurt those who are weaker. It's true physically, and it's true emotionally. If you're ever in a confrontation where you could verbally or intellectually destroy the person who disagrees with you, gentleness prevents you from doing so. Gentleness means you don't get in someone's face and yell. People are fragile; they need to be handled with care.

Gentleness in reaction

Life is 10% about what happens to you and 90% of how you react. Sometimes you have no control over what happens to you, but when you surrender to Jesus you can control your emotions.

Before he met Jesus, the Apostle Paul was a hothead. He approved the stoning of Stephen, and he viciously attacked other Christians and had them arrested and thrown in prison. But when He met Jesus on the road to Damascus, he received a personality transplant.

One of the most dysfunctional churches Paul founded was at Corinth. They had all kinds of problems, from practicing sexual immorality to needlessly suing each other. Some of the members were critical of Paul, saying he wasn't really an apostle anyway and that no one should listen to him. When Paul wrote to them to address these problems, he was not happy. He asked, "What do you prefer? Shall I come to you with a whip, or in love and with a gentle spirit?" (1 Corinthians 4:21) In the end, however, he didn't choose the whip; he chose love. If you don't believe it, just read the thirteenth chapter of his letter to these messed-up believers. We often call it the Love Chapter.

GENTLENESS

123

Jesus also reacted in gentleness when He was insulted. First Peter 2:23 says, "When they hurled their insults at him, he did not retaliate; when he suffered, he made no threats." In Luke 9 Jesus and His disciples made plans to enter a Samaritan village and spend the night. But the Samaritans refused to show them hospitality. Suddenly every Holiday Inn sign read, "No vacancy." All the Samaritan restaurant owners said, "Sorry, no Jews allowed." James and John, nicknamed "the Sons of Thunder," were so infuriated by this unfair treatment that they wanted Jesus to call down fire from heaven and burn up those sorry Samaritans. Could Jesus have called down fire? Absolutely! Did He? No. Instead, He rebuked them and reminded them that He did not come to destroy people's lives but to save them.

How do you react when people attack you or say something unfair? How do you respond when a stranger makes a snide remark? When they cut you off in traffic? The *easiest* thing to do is to react with anger and hostility. But if you are full of Jesus, then you will react with gentleness. People are fragile—they need to be handled with care.

Gentleness in words

One of the greatest needs in our world today is for us to *speak* with greater gentleness to one another. There is so much hatred and animosity, and it is downright scary sometimes. Profanity has become the norm rather than the exception. It reminds me of the story about when a preacher responded to an ad for a used lawn mower. When he got to the home that was selling the equipment, he was surprised to see a little boy was standing outside waiting to show it to him. The preacher looked at the mower and then leaned over it and asked the boy, "Can I try to start it?"

The boy agreed, so the preacher grabbed the cord and pulled it, but the engine didn't start. After a few hard pulls and nothing happening, the boy said, "My daddy says you have to cuss at it to get it to start."

The preacher said, "Well, I'm a preacher and I haven't cussed in 18 years."

The boy did not miss a beat. He said, "Keep on pulling the rope. It'll come back to you."

Most people who know me consider me to be a calm guy. But I used to have a terrible temper. In high school I was so competitive that I would often lose my temper and say things I shouldn't have said. It didn't take much to cause me to fly into a rage. I was ejected from at least two high school basketball games for losing my cool with the referees.

But when I got to college, God convicted me that if I was going to be a pastor, I had to get rid of my anger. I wrote a verse of Scripture on an index card and taped it to the mirror in my dorm room. Every time I looked in the mirror, I would quote Proverbs 15:1. It says, "A gentle answer turns away wrath, but a harsh word stirs up anger." God used that one verse to harness my anger.

Is that a verse you need to write down and keep before your eyes on a regular basis? God can use that simple truth to transform your personality like He did mine.

Sometimes it's not the words we say, but the tone of voice we use. A man attended a wedding and afterward he told a friend he didn't think the marriage would last. His friend asked him why he felt that way. He said, "Well, when the groom said, 'I do' the bride retorted, 'Don't use that tone of voice with me!'"

HOW you say something is at least as important as WHAT you say. For instance, imagine two people who are arguing with each other. Finally, one person decides to apologize and sincerely says, "I am so sorry." But what if that person were to utter the same words with a different tone of voice? You've probably heard people issue an apology in a mocking tone of voice that sounds like, "WELL! I'm soooo sorry." They're not sorry at all! They're not handling the other person with care.

The Bible says the tongue has tremendous power. James wrote, "Likewise the tongue is a small part of the body, but it makes great boasts. Consider what a great forest is set on fire by a small spark. The tongue also is a fire, a world of evil among the parts of the body. It corrupts the whole person, sets the whole course of his life on fire, and is itself set on fire by hell." (James 3:5–6) Wow. That's powerful.

Fire can be a good thing if it is kept under control. It can heat a cold house and cook a delicious meal. But the annual wildfires on the West Coast remind us that uncontrolled fire can cause widespread devastation. A forest fire never begins with a forest on fire; it starts with a spark. You can use one little word from your tongue to delight or to destroy. People are fragile—handle them with care.

Meek, Not Weak

One of my favorite sports heroes was Coach John Wooden, head basketball coach for the UCLA Bruins in the 1970s. His team set records that will never be broken. It's hard to win one national championship, and he won seven in a row. Not only that, he also won a total of 10 national championships in a 12-year period. And his team won 88 games in a row!

Some coaches, like Bobby Knight, are known for their fiery style. But John Wooden was one of the most gentle men who ever lived. Although he was intense during games, his strongest expletive was, "My goodness gracious." He had a reputation for molding players with rough personalities like Bill Walton into team players and winners.

In his autobiography Wooden wrote that as a young man he had a volatile temper. But his dad, Joshua, had a profound impact on him. He said his dad was one of the strongest men he'd ever known, able to lift weights men half his age couldn't budge. But he was gentle and even read poetry to his children at night. Coach Wooden recalled an incident in his childhood:

"We had a team of mules named Jack and Kate. Kate would often get stubborn and lie down on me when I was plowing. I couldn't get her up no matter how roughly I whipped her or yelled at her. Dad would see my predicament and walk across the field and lean down and rub Kate's ear gently and say, 'Come on, Kate.' She would get up and start walking again. He never touched her in anger. It took me a long time to understand that even a stubborn mule responds to gentleness. My dad taught me that it takes a lot of strength on the inside to be gentle on the outside."

The reason John Wooden was a gentle man is because He allowed Jesus to be gentle in him. He said of his faith: "I have always tried to make it clear that basketball is not the ultimate. It is of small importance in comparison to the total life we live. There is only one kind of life that truly wins, and that is the one that places faith in the hands of the Savior."

Will you allow the Holy Spirit to infuse your personality with the gentleness of Jesus? We don't use "meek" as a verb in English, but have you allowed the Holy Spirit to "meek" you? Is your will still unbroken and your behavior unbridled? The Bible teaches that God treasures brokenness in a person. After King David had confessed sin in his life he wrote, "The sacrifices of God are a broken spirit; a broken and contrite heart, O God, you will not despise." (Psalm 51:17) Remember, people are fragile—they need to be handled with care!

TAKEAWAY TRUTH
Put What You Are Learning Into Practice

I want to issue a gentleness challenge. Why don't you declare the next seven days as Meek Week? For the next seven days, allow the gentleness of Jesus to be displayed in your life as you relate to your family, your friends, at work, or at school. At the end of the week, reflect on how you feel, what you did differently, and how people responded to you.

CHAPTER 10

Self-Control: Who's In Charge Here?

ove is the first flavor of the fruit of the Spirit and in this chapter we come to the last in the list: self-control. I think these two virtues are placed first and last like bookends. Love is the primary fruit that empowers the rest of the character traits, and self-control is the virtue that holds them all together.

Some people have a reputation of being control freaks. They want to control everything in life except themselves. There are many things in life you can't control. For instance, you can't control the weather. When someone says, "Pastor we're having an outside event will you ask the Lord for good weather that day?" I always say, "Sorry, but I'm in sales, not management!"

And even though you may try, you can't control other people.

A bride-to-be was so nervous and didn't think she could make it down the aisle. Her maid of honor said, "Just focus on three things. Look down at the aisle and walk. Then look up at the altar where the preacher is standing. And then look at your groom." So the bride decided to remember those three things. As she walked down the aisle she was even saying in a quiet voice, "Aisle. Altar. Him."

As much as we try to alter and control our spouses, children, friends, and co-workers, we can't. But with the power of the Holy Spirit you can exercise control over the person who gives you the most trouble: You. I saw a sign recently with a quote from Teddy Roosevelt that made me laugh. It said: "If you could kick the person in the pants responsible for most of your trouble, you wouldn't sit for a month."

Before we go any further into this chapter, why don't you raise your right hand and confess this vow: **"With God's help, I will stop trying to control other people and things over which I have no control."** Good. Now you're ready to learn about the most important kind of control: Self-control. Let's start by answering some important questions.

IS ANY AREA OF MY LIFE OUT OF CONTROL?

Everybody struggles with self-control. We all wish we had more of it. One of our members who teaches at a Christian school told me the true story of a first-grader in her school who had been taken out in the hall by his teacher because he was disrupting the class.

Since they are a Christian school, the teacher spoke to him about the importance of the fruit of the Spirit. She began to name them all, and when she got to self-control the little boy held up his hand and said, "Hold it right there. That's the one I have trouble with." Well, join the rest of us because all of us struggle with self-control. We all wish we had more of it.

To see if there are areas where you might need more self-control let me ask you three questions about areas that can get out of control.

Do you have any uncontrolled appetites?

God has given us appetites for food, drink, pleasure, love, acceptance, and many other things that we crave. But God has also given us normal, healthy ways to satisfy these appetites. The world, our flesh, and the devil want you to overindulge your appetites.

The Bible says, "When you sit down to eat with a ruler, consider carefully what is before you; And put a knife to your throat if you are a man given to great appetite." (Proverbs 23:1–2 NASB)

A lack of control means that you want something and you've got to have it NOW! How much self-control do you have? Can you practice delayed gratification, or do you have to have it all right now? In 1972 social experiments on self-control were conducted at Stanford University. Researchers selected 600 four-year-olds and put each child in a room with a single marshmallow in front of them. The children were told that if they could wait 15 minutes and not eat the marshmallow, then they would be rewarded with another marshmallow. The dilemma each child faced is the same thing we face every day. "Do I eat the one marshmallow NOW, or do I wait and get twice as many?" Of the 600 children, only 30% of them were able to wait.

But that wasn't the point of the experiment. The researchers followed the developmental progress of the same children into adolescence and young adulthood. The 30% who practiced self-control were better adjusted socially, more dependable, and in high school scored significantly higher on their SAT college entrance exam. What's the point of the marshmallow test? Self-control impacts every area of your life.

Do you have any uncontrolled ambition?

Sometimes we try to bite off more than we can chew. There's nothing wrong with ambition. We should all be ambitious to please God and serve God. But ambition has a dark side when it becomes selfish. Galatians 5:20 contains the opposite list of the fruit of the Spirit—I call this list "the weeds of the devil." One of the sins of the flesh listed is "selfish ambition." The Bible says, "Do nothing out of selfish ambition or vain conceit, but in humility consider others better than yourselves. Each of you should look not only to your own interests, but also to the interests of others." (Philippians 2:3–4)

Can you think of a Bible character who had uncontrolled ambition? How about King David's son Absalom? The Bible says he was extremely handsome and vain. He had such thick hair that when he cut it each year, he would weigh it. Who does that? He would have become king when his father died, but that wasn't soon enough for him. So Absalom hatched a sinister plot to steal the throne. He enlisted 50 soldiers to go before him like a celebrity entourage and applaud him everywhere he went. Absalom would also station himself at the gates of the city to kiss babies and talk about what a terrible king David was. In other words, he was a born politician.

After a few months of this crusade of criticism, most people decided they wanted Absalom as king, so he attempted a hostile takeover. But instead of fighting his son, David was heartbroken and vacated Jerusalem. He left town barefoot and weeping with a few of his faithful men. Even so, Absalom and his soldiers pursued them.

In the heat of the battle Absalom was riding a mule that ducked under the tangled branches of an oak tree. His pride became his downfall as his thick hair got caught in the limbs. The mule kept going and left Absalom hanging there. Talk about a bad hair day! David didn't want to harm his son, but his general, Joab, didn't feel the same way. When he found Absalom hanging there, he threw three spears into Absalom's heart. When David heard about his son's death, he cried, "Oh my son Absalom, if only I had died instead of you!" (2 Samuel 18:33) It's tough for parents to bury children, even rebellious ones. Absalom's greedy ambition got him in the end.

We live in a nation where most people only want one thing: MORE. They want more power, more food, more drink, more money, more toys, more cars, more channels, more pornography, more thrills, more perks, and more success. A few years ago a survey asked Americans across all economic levels how much money it would take to make them happy. Not a single person responded that they were happy with what they had. Instead, everyone answered an amount that was more than what they were currently making.

Do you have uncontrolled anger?

Anger is not a sin, but uncontrolled, raging anger is. The Bible says in Ephesians 4:26, "In your anger do not sin. Do not let the sun go down while you are still angry."

In 1978 the Ohio State Buckeyes, coached by Woody Hayes, were playing Clemson in the Gator Bowl. At that time, he was one of the most respected football coaches in the nation and had led the Buckeyes to five national championships. But today he isn't remembered for all the wins he coached but for a single, spectacular moment when he didn't control his anger. In the fourth quarter of the Gator Bowl, Charlie Bauman, the Clemson nose guard, intercepted a pass from the Ohio State quarterback. As he was returning the interception, he ran out of bounds on the Ohio State sidelines. In front of a national television audience, Woody Hayes lost his temper and grabbed Bauman by the helmet and started punching him in the throat. That led to a bench-clearing brawl. The next day Coach Hayes was fired. He died nine years later but never apologized to Bauman.

The Bible says, "A quick-tempered man does foolish things, and a crafty man is hated." (Proverbs 14:17) When you lose your temper, you lose more than just that. You could lose your job, lose your family, and lose the respect of other people. Permanently.

LACK OF SELF-CONTROL LEADS TO RUIN
If you never practice self-control, your life may spin out of control.

MEMORIZE THIS

"Like a city whose walls are broken down is a man who lacks self-control." (Proverbs 25:28)

In ancient times, cities had walls around them to protect them from attackers. When the walls were broken down, there was no way to protect the city and it would usually end up in ruins. Do you have some strong walls in your life? Do you have solid boundaries? Have you built margin into your personal life, or are you living on the edge?

Can you think of another Bible character who had little or no self-control? Absalom wasn't the only one who had a bad hair day. Samson had one, too. He was born to godly parents, and he took a Nazarite vow not to cut his hair and to live a pure life. His strength wasn't in his hair; it was in his commitment to God.

But Samson forgot about his vow and lived a reckless life with no boundaries. He was a he-man with a she-problem. Delilah pretended to love him, but she was a secret agent for the Philistines. God gave Samson supernatural strength, but Delilah did not know that. She begged Samson to reveal the source of his strength, and he tricked her several times by giving her false information. First he said, "Tie me up with strings from a bow and I'll be as weak as a puppy." While he was sleeping, she did just that. When the Philistine soldiers came in she said, "Samson, the Philistines are here!" Samson jumped up and broke those strings like they were spider webs and killed all the Philistines.

Delilah did not give up. She kept pouting and pleading, and one day he said, "Take new ropes and bind me and I'll be as weak as a puppy." While he was snoring, she signaled the soldiers and they pounced on Samson. But he woke up and killed them all.

After another lie, finally Samson revealed the truth. He said that a razor had never touched his hair, and if he was shaved, he would be as weak as a puppy. Once again while he was asleep, she shaved his head. His strength really wasn't in his long hair; it was in his commitment to God, remember. But when the final symbol of his commitment was cut off, his supernatural strength left as well.

The biblical account of his life reveals what happened. Delilah said,

"'Samson, the Philistines are upon you!' He awoke from his sleep, and thought, 'I will go out as before and shake myself free.' But he did not know that the Lord had left him. Then the Philistines seized him, gouged out his eyes and took him down to Gaza. Binding him with bronze shackles, they set him to grinding in the prison." (Judges 16:20–21) The saddest part of that story for me is that Samson fully expected the power of God to be there, but it was gone. He traveled down the long slippery slope of losing self-control and finding oneself without the power of God. That's what people discover at the end of forgetting their commitment to God.

SURRENDER CONTROL OF "SELF"

You and I can never control "self" in our own strength. My only hope is to surrender my sinful self to Jesus who lives in me. In Luke 9:23 Jesus said, "If anyone would come after me, he must deny himself and take up his cross daily and follow me." That doesn't mean that you deny yourself something like chocolate; it means that you deny SELF or your sinful nature. It's the part of your personality that always says, "Gimme, gimme, gimme."

Who's in charge in your life? You or Jesus? I was in a store not long ago and watched as an obviously spoiled little boy pointed to some candy and yelled, "Mommy, Mommy, I want that!" His mother said, "No, you don't need that." At this, he started screaming and stomping his little feet. He whined, "I want it and I want it NOW!" Then I watched as the harried mother quickly grabbed the chocolate and said, "Here, now please stop crying." I wanted to say, "Excuse me, but who's in charge around here?"

Each of us has that little boy inside of us—it's called SELF. I wonder if the Lord doesn't look at us with frustration sometimes when we neglect His Word and insist on doing our own thing. Can you hear Him asking, "Who's in charge around here?" Self-control simply means saying, "Lord, I know what I want. But You're in charge of my life." That's what it means to daily deny self and take up your cross. What happens when we surrender control of our lives to Jesus?

Jesus in me—will say no to the wrong things!

When Ronald Reagan was our President, his wife Nancy took a leading role in the war against drugs. She was at an elementary school in San Diego when a schoolgirl asked her what she should do if someone offered her drugs. Without thinking, Nancy Reagan said, "Why, you just say 'no.'" That statement launched a campaign called "Just Say No to Drugs." As a result, thousands of schools established "Just Say No" clubs where students made a pledge not to experiment with drugs.

That's a wonderful idea, but the problem with just saying no to drugs is that most people don't have the willpower to just say no to a Krispy Kreme donut. It's not as easy as JUST saying no. Our willpower isn't strong enough. God told Adam and Eve, "Just say NO to the forbidden fruit." And you see how that worked out for all of us!

Each of us needs a supernatural power within us giving us the strength to say no. And that's what Jesus does when you surrender control of your life to Him. That's the inside job. The Bible says, "For the grace of God that brings salvation has appeared to all men. It teaches us to say 'no' to ungodliness and worldly passions and to live self-controlled, upright and godly lives in this present age." (Titus

2:11–12) But self-control isn't merely saying, "No" to the wrong things. We have to say "Yes" to the right things.

Jesus in me—will say yes to the right things!

We all love to hear the word, "Yes!" When you're applying for a job, or a scholarship, or when you propose to someone you want to marry, you want to hear, "Yes!" I've often said God's favorite word is, "Yes." Most people think of God as a mean cosmic schoolteacher who's ready to slap your wrist with a ruler and say, "No, no, no!" But the Bible says, "For no matter how many promises God has made, they are 'yes' in Christ." (2 Corinthians 1:20)

The struggle with your sinful nature isn't a matter of listening to a bad angel on one shoulder and a good angel on the other. As followers of Jesus Christ, we have another option. Jesus lives in you, and He always says, "Yes" to the right things and "No" to the wrong things. So the only thing we need to say "Yes" to is this: "YES, Jesus, I surrender my 'self' to your control!" The choice we have isn't about doing wrong or right; it's the choice about whether or not we will allow Jesus to make that choice for us.

When I was in college, someone explained it to me by sharing an evangelistic booklet called a tract written by Campus Crusade for Christ. It was entitled, *"Have you made the Wonderful Discovery of the Spirit-filled life?"* I was a Christian, but I was trying to live the Christian life in my own strength. The truth was that I was in charge of my life, not Christ. This friend showed me a circle that represented my life. A big "S" representing "self" was on a throne. Then there was another circle beside it with "self" off the throne and a cross, representing Jesus, seated instead on the throne.

My friend asked me, "Which circle best represents your life right now?" I pointed to the one with the big S on the throne. I was clearly in charge of my life. He then asked, "Which circle represents how you'd like to live?" And I pointed to the one with the cross on the throne. I really wanted Christ to be in charge of my daily life. I then prayed a simple prayer where I asked Jesus to sit on the throne of my life. It was a turning point because for the first time I understood what it meant to let Jesus be the king of my life. The prayer I prayed that night wasn't a once-for-all prayer. Jesus said we must DAILY deny self and take up the cross.

Until that time, it was as if my life was a car and Jesus had been a passenger. He was in my life, but I had the steering wheel. I'd sometimes see a detour and flip on the blinker and Jesus would say, "Don't go down that road!" I'd say, "Who's driving? Me or you?" Then I'd always end up lost and stuck in the mud of my poor decisions. Then I'd say, "Jesus please give me directions to get back on the main road."

My life was a continual series of bad detours. But on that night, I truly surrendered to Jesus as Lord. I said, "Jesus, let's swap places. I want You to have the steering wheel." At that moment I became the passenger, and He became the driver. Through the years I've seen plenty of flashing billboards directing me to go down the wrong road, and I've leaned over to Jesus and said, "Hey, what about that? Let's try that road!" And Jesus simply says in reply, "Who's driving? Me or you?"

The first president I can remember knowing about was Dwight David Eisenhower. He was a great leader and I really liked Ike. Before he was elected president, he was the Supreme Commander of the

Allied Forces in WWII and planned and carried out the invasion of Northern Africa in 1942 and then the Normandy Invasion in 1945. He was a great leader who captured enemy cities, but he never would have been able to lead men into battle if he hadn't learned an important lesson about self-control early in his life.

Ike was born in Denton, Texas, but he grew up on a farm in Kansas where his parents prayed and read the Bible at breakfast and at dinner. Ike had five brothers and no sisters, and they were always fighting. Young Ike developed a terrible temper and he would often fly into a blind rage. One Halloween his father refused to let him go trick-or-treating with his older brothers and he was so mad he went outside and started pounding his fists into the bark of a tree. He kept hitting until his hands were bleeding. His father pulled him back into the house and spanked him.

Later his mother came to Ike's room to take care of him. After she finished bandaging his bleeding hands she took her Bible and read a verse of Scripture to Ike that he would never forget. It was Proverbs 16:32 which says, "He who is slow to anger is better than the mighty; and he who rules his spirit than he who takes a city." (Proverbs 16:32)

Dwight Eisenhower said from that point in his life he made a settled decision that with God's strength he would control his anger, rather than letting his anger control him. Who knows where he would have ended up without self-control? Who knows where our nation might be now if he hadn't been a man who demonstrated the spiritual fruit of self-control?

So, let me ask you, when it comes to your life, "Who's in charge around here?" If you answered, "Jesus is!" Then you're on the blessed road of self-control and all the other fruit of the Spirit with it. God can and will transform your personality over time until you are reflecting the personality of His Son, Jesus Christ.

TAKEAWAY TRUTH

Put What You Are Learning Into Practice

Over the next 30 days, pray through the list of the fruit of the Spirit in Galatians 5 one-by-one each day. Ask God to deepen His work inside of your heart and personality so that these traits become part of who you are. At the end of 30 days, reflect back on how you've already started to grow. Then start over again for the next 30 days! It's a long road ahead—but with His power and your willingness to surrender to Him, that road will lead you to be the person you're meant to be.

"But the fruit of the Spirit is love, joy, peace, patience, kindness, goodness, faithfulness, gentleness and self-control. Against such things there is no law. Those who belong to Christ Jesus have crucified the sinful nature with its passions and desires. Since we live by the Spirit, let us keep in step with the Spirit."

GALATIANS 5:22–25

For more information,
visit www.NcourageResources.org

9 781732 855717